Unconsolable Contemporary

Unconsolable Contemporary

Contemporary

Observing Gerhard Richter | **PAUL RABINOW**

Duke University Press   Durham and London   2017

Designed by Heather Hensley
Typeset in Minion and Meta by Tseng Information Systems, Inc.

Library of Congress Cataloging-in-Publication Data
Names: Rabinow, Paul, author.
Title: Unconsolable contemporary : observing Gerhard Richter /
Paul Rabinow.
Description: Durham : Duke University Press, 2017.
Includes bibliographical references and index.
Identifiers: LCCN 2017035991 (print) | LCCN 2017040729 (ebook) |
ISBN 9780822372271 (ebook) | ISBN 9780822369967 (hardcover : alk.
paper) | ISBN 9780822370017 (pbk. : alk. paper)
Subjects: LCSH: Richter, Gerhard, 1932 — Criticism and interpretation. |
Philosophical anthropology. | Art and philosophy.
Classification: LCC ND588.R48 (ebook)
LCC ND588.R48 R335 2017 (print) DDC 709.2 — dc23
LC record available at https://lccn.loc.gov/2017035991

Cover art: Gerhard Richter at work. Photograph by Benjamin Katz.
Courtesy of Benjamin Katz and the Gerhard Richter Archive.

To Anthony Stavrianakis

For with friends men are better able both to think and to do.
It is those who wish the good for their friends for their
friends' sake who are friends most truly.

—ARISTOTLE, *Nicomachean Ethics* (1155b, 16–17; 1156b, 8–10)

CONTENTS

1   **INTRODUCTION**
Form and Birkenau

15   **CHAPTER 1**
Object: The Contemporary

33   **CHAPTER 2**
Constellations: Writing and Imaging Strife

65   **CHAPTER 3**
Assembling: Abet and Facilitate

95   **CHAPTER 4**
Composition: *Technē* and Pathos

125   **CHAPTER 5**
Contemporary Consolations: Unconsoled

141   **CHAPTER 6**
Restive Endings

NOTES **147**   BIBLIOGRAPHY **159**

INTRODUCTION   Form and Birkenau

> One readily believes that a culture is more attached to its values
> than to its forms; that the latter can be easily modified, aban-
> doned, reworked; that it is only meaning that is deeply rooted.
> This would be to misunderstand how much forms, when they
> come apart or when they are born, can provoke astonishment
> or hate; it is to misunderstand that people hold dearly to their
> ways of seeing, of saying, of doing and of thinking, more than
> what one sees, says and does. The battle of forms in the West
> has been hard fought, if not more than that of ideas and values.
> This battle has taken a singular shape in the twentieth century:
> it is "the formal" itself, it is the reflective work on the system of
> forms that has become the stakes of the battle. Form has become
> a remarkable object of moral hostilities, aesthetic debates and
> political confrontations.
> —**Michel Foucault**

The core intent of this work is to invent, test, and practice one form of the
interplay of inquiry and narration. During the course of the narrative, the
reader will encounter a series of observations principally (but not uniquely)
concerning the German artist Gerhard Richter. As I am neither an art historian nor an art critic nor a cultural studies specialist, my contribution is best
characterized as an amateur one, albeit an anthropological one. For a range
of reasons that I will explore as this work unfolds, I have been "taken" by
Gerhard Richter, his artistic production, and the assemblage of critics asso-

ciated with it and with him, as well as the apparatuses of the institutions of the art world and the theory world with their currently ever-expanding markets of material and symbolic goods.

Given that I am currently, and have for some time now, been thinking, observing, and writing about Gerhard Richter, the question arises: Why focus on this artist? Engaging Richter is a form of disciplinary trespassing that one allows oneself from time to time and at a certain age. Consequently, the simplest answer is that Gerhard Richter makes available for reflection, through his work and his practice, one form of an ethos of the contemporary.

For me the stakes of taking up Gerhard Richter is neither that his work is a special instance of current trends in painting or the art world more broadly nor that it serves as an example drawn to buttress a theory of contemporary painting. To the contrary, one of the most compelling things about Gerhard Richter to me is that he can be seen to embody what Gilles Deleuze names as "a singular life."[1] Hence taking Richter up as an exemplar of his historical period, or as someone doing precisely the same thing as what we as anthropologists of the contemporary are seeking to do, is not only futile; it is at best a betrayal of his singularity as well as of our uncertain efforts to articulate and test the elements of an anthropology of the contemporary, and, at worst, merely crude or as Kant might well have added, "lazy and cowardly."[2]

The problem at hand is: why (and how to) establish a relationship to Richter's practice and production? One simple answer is that we are contemporaries in the standard meaning of the term—we are both living at the same time. That being said, Richter is German, an artist who is at least one momentous generation older; he has lived through a significant set of historical experiences none of which overlap directly with my own or those of my generation yet are not so far removed or different so as to render them exotic or beyond comprehension. Richter's singularity is not fundamentally Other. Perhaps Richter's experiences, his art, his location, his ethos, his practice of discourse and rendering things visible provide a rich repertoire of the recent past (its problems, multiple responses). In fact, it is his very singularity that opens the possibility of non-identification and consequently of adjacency.

One of Richter's practices is to be receptive to interviews, a practice he has entertained and honed for decades now. Many of these are published in his increasingly large volume of writings almost all of which consist in interviews and letters.[3] Richter does not write treatises or art criticism. He is carefully silent about his personal life although his interactions and interventions with historical trends and events is a topic he is willing to discuss. He has however surrounded himself with a range of people who do write treatises and art criticism for a living. Several of these people also curate exhibitions.

Entering into this circle of critics seems to require some time and patience; familiarity and trust between the artist and those who he allows to interview him has yielded a series of privileged interlocutors: Benjamin Buchloh, Robert Storr, and Hans-Ulrich Obrist. Perhaps we could say that Richter has engaged a series of critics and curators of modern art; we should ponder the possibility that such a practice is significant, that it itself constitutes an important element in a contemporary ethos. To explore that possibility requires being attentive to the manner in which Richter frames the interviews and the quality of the responses he characteristically provides, refuses, evades, or muses upon.

Whatever else Richter's coy interviews are "really" about, one thing is clear: how to improve—or to judge—his image-making in either a technical sense or even an aesthetic one, is practically nonexistent as a topic. Rather, his "intentions," his "interventions," his "reactions," his "opinions," are queried; encouraging his interlocutors to raise these topics apparently helps Richter understand some range of reaction to his work. Perhaps they are part pedagogic (an artist interested in a strange theoretic discourse), in part strategic (cultivating critics and curators who are making his work public and its reception channeled), in part contributing to his practice of image-making although this third ramification is basically never thematized.

That being said, my relationship with Richter is neither one of identity nor one of identification. Richter has few imitators (none prominent); there is no school or style attached to his name. What captures and concentrates my interest in this regard is the constitution of an assemblage of heterogeneous elements; how it is brought into play; how it is kept in motion; the distinct distances that are kept tensile among and between domains and discourses; the restive and recalcitrant ethos that Richter has harnessed and that animates things.

Thus, at a surface level, this book is about the ongoing experiments of artistic practice as well as about those attempting to say what is going on in such practice. My goal is not to engage directly on either of these registers in their own terms but rather my intent is to produce a second-order anthropological account that takes these registers seriously—from a position of adjacency. Thus, its concern is how to see and to narrate the 'becoming historical' of what had been taken to be seeable and enunciable for certain self-styled modernists.

Finally, neither the practitioners nor the anthropologist give credence to the existence of an epochal "post-modern," if by that one means the overcoming in a definitive fashion of what has been taken to be the defining elements of the modern project in the arts as well as in thought. Rather, it attempts to forge one way of rendering visible and enunciable a specific reflective relation to the present thereby configuring it as actual. Let's call this process one of forging a contemporary ethos.[4]

Although the bulk of the book concerns the work of Gerhard Richter and a few artists (Alexander Kluge, Pierre Boulez, and others), it is nonetheless intended as an exercise in a contemporary anthropology. One might say the book *concerns* artistic practice and the particular discourses that surround it. That being said, however, the book's work is *about* second-order observations of such assemblages and how they can be indexed, at least implicitly, to a larger problematization. Assembling the *concern* and the *about* provide parameters for an experiment in a contemporary anthropology as well as an anthropology of the contemporary.

Form

One can readily agree with Foucault that during the twentieth century the status of form (or 'the formal') was the site of high-stakes battles. These battles and their presumed stakes were potently charged in the moral, aesthetic, and political realms. Let us call the site of these debates and creations over form—*modernism*.

Of course, during the course of what one might call 'the long twentieth century' there were also, innumerable, concurrent, and at times over-lapping and at times not, confrontations and experiments concerning values and ideas. Max Weber, identified the separation of value spheres—the moral, the aesthetic, and the political—as the defining diacritic of *modernity*.

There has been, and continues to be, much confusion as to what the relations of the modern and modernity have been and should be. Nonetheless drawing an analytic distinction between them is helpful in orienting what follows. Be forewarned, I do not intend to enter directly into the thicket of issues encompassed by the vast literature on these subjects. This book is not a treatise. Rather, in what I think of as an anthropological fashion—the tentative twining of conceptual work and empirical materials through inquiry—I will explore the experiments of Gerhard Richter as an object of study as well as a source of insight and inspiration concerning the status of the modern and modernity and their ramifications and reconfigurations in the present.

In order to do so, I have invented the term *the contemporary* that I have defined as follows: "Just as the 'modern' can be thought of as a moving ratio of tradition and modernity, so the contemporary 'is a moving ratio of modernity, moving through the recent past and near future in a (non-linear) space.'"[5]

I will utilize a term taken from the German art historian Aby Warburg—*Nachleben* (afterlife, survival)[6]—to situate what I take to be a plausible manner of taking up Richter's practices as a contemporary ethos. One could say Richter acknowledges modernist theory concerning modern art as something that an artist in the late twentieth century has had to come to terms with while letting it be part of what I will argue is—to use a second borrowing from Warburg to which I return below—the *Pathosformel* (form given to pathos),[7] which Richter has inventively integrated into his own image-making and practice.

The manner in which Richter has given form to the challenge of modernism and modernity over the course of decades is best approached, I believe, through a form of chronicle. The chronicle turns on what I consider to be the manner in which Richter has taken up the modern and modernity as inevitable aspects of his work but has found or sought a means of shifting their framing as historical but not determinative of the problem-space of painting. I call that ceaseless experimentation an ethos of the contemporary. There is no postmodern for Richter; rather, there is what, following Aby Warburg and Georges Didi-Huberman, we can call "the afterlife of the modern" (*Nachleben der Moderne*).[8]

Richter himself remains elusive, and at times simply evasive, as to his positions, if any, on values, ideas, and politics. That being said, one of the aspects of Richter's practice that I find highly innovative is precisely the form he has developed of dealing with these domains. Over the course of decades, Richter has cultivated a practice of interviews with learned and theoretically oriented interlocutors. By so doing, Richter makes it clear that he is aware of the stakes attributed to these domains and their discussions and arguments, but he also makes it clear that as a painter his overriding concern, and ultimately his responsibility, is to paint.

It will not have escaped the astute reader's attention that Michel Foucault himself deployed the interview form to similar ends, albeit fashioned to meet his own highly distinctive purposes. After the frustrations and dissatisfactions arising from his one main attempt to theorize his own practice, *The Archaeology of Knowledge*, Foucault adopted a critical stance of refusing such theorizing as a matter of principle—and of form. As the demand to explicate his positions on ideas, values, and politics was constant, Foucault responded during the last two decades of his life by adopting the interview form and shaping it to his own ends both as a refusal and as a tentative site of testing for himself and others. He felt freer to offer opinions, at times judgments, at other times snippets of autobiography, always in a conditional mode and always separate from his experiments in form in his books and essays.

I too, naturally in a more modest manner, have turned to interviews for some of the same reasons. Humbling or humiliating comparisons aside, it seems to me that contemporary anthropology for the last several decades has, in a haphazard and uncoordinated fashion, been in search of formal innovation. In my view, the field has not fulfilled the promises of *Writing Culture: The Politics and Poetics of Ethnography* (1986) to experiment with and to establish narrative and media forms adequate to our times.[9] In that light, while hoping for better days and attempting to make my own contributions, I have turned to those like Foucault, Richter, and Roland Barthes who—while being keenly aware of and attentive to the stakes of debates and contests of aesthetics, ideas, and politics—have shown us different manners of formal experimentation or experiments in form. I have sought to learn from these experiments—not, of course, to imitate them but to become more attentive to the diverse challenges and different projects taking shape within a problem-space whose contours, limits, and richness we lack the tools to adequately conceptualize. It is in that light that I conceived of this book not as an essay in ethnography but rather as an anthropological test.

Kairos l

In 2014, Gerhard Richter exhibited a series of paintings (and photographic reproductions of the abstract paintings) as part of a larger exhibition in Dresden under the title "abstract paintings." In 2015 he exhibited the paintings and photo reproductions alone in Baden-Baden and this time he gave them the highly resonant name "Birkenau." He also published a book of sixty-three small-format plates, sections of the paintings without any commentary. In 2015, the art critic Benjamin H. D. Buchloh published an essay (in book form with plates) entitled *Gerhard Richters* Birkenau-*Bilder*.[10] Buchloh, Richter's most theoretically sophisticated interlocutor and interviewer, is a distinguished German historian of art and holds the position of Andrew W. Mellon Professor of Modern Art at Harvard. Richter refers to Buchloh as his friend, and there is even a portrait painted by Richter of the two of them side by side. While not explicitly authorized by the artist, *Gerhard Richters* Birkenau-*Bilder* nonetheless was clearly done in cooperation with the artist. Hence, here as elsewhere, the special friendship and access that Buchloh enjoys with Richter provides his interpretations with a prima facie authority. Throughout my book, I concur that Buchloh's views must be taken into account as a significant dimension of the form Richter is developing. Such acknowledgment, of course, does not impose agreement with Buchloh's value positions on aesthetics, morals, and politics, only how Richter gives them form.

As we will also see throughout the course of this book, Buchloh plays a distinctive role of posing questions and interpretations to Richter, often in the high jargon of the Frankfurt School or the journal *October*, perhaps the leading theory journal of the art world for several decades. Buchloh is an associate editor and on the editorial committee as is his thesis adviser, Rosalind Krauss. Richter's responses to Buchloh's questions and interpretations will also play an important role in this narrative as Richter often, very often, expresses a lack of understanding of the questions posed or simply disagrees. I argue that this fact is significant as it seems to illustrate Richter's awareness of the place of modernist discourse in the art world as well as his means of distancing himself from it.

Amnesia and Anamnesis?

In his book on the Birkenau paintings, Buchloh poses the following question, in a fashion typical of his prose and rhetoric: "Can a German artist construct a credible mnemonic representation of the Holocaust with painterly or photographic means?"[11] He then describes how this question or a variant of this challenge has been acutely present for Richter for half a century. The argument is that, for Richter, the Holocaust was the *kairos*—the turning point of the highest significance—with which he had to come to terms.

Buchloh argues that Richter felt compelled, even obliged, to find or invent some form of image for the camps. One alternative was to refuse any image-making, and thereby to respond to the *kairos* by consciously choosing to attempt "any form of an iconically mediated reception of the unrepresentable, and therefore to delegitimate any of these attempts."[12]

This choice was not one Richter would ever settle on.

Wasn't his dilemma, Buchloh wonders, at the heart of all of Richter's painterly production? "The artist returned to the question repeatedly over five decades, and his response remained equally constant in erasing the possibility and negating the credibility of any iconic representation."[13]

This fact does demonstrate an enduring thematic concern, one not at all uncommon for German artists and thinkers as well as for many others both within Germany and beyond, but the stronger claim that it constitutes the heart of Richter's art in a totalizing manner is contestable. Richter's work is both broader and deeper than his timely attempts to come to terms with the Nazis. I am arguing instead that Richter's *kairos* was the relationship of modernism to modernity as they became historical but with a vivid and haunting afterlife.

Versions

Richter's first attempt to come to terms artistically with the Holocaust was during the years 1965–67; it is documented in Richter's long-standing collection of an orderly array of photo reproductions, periodically updated in print, the *Atlas*. According to Buchloh, the effort originated at the time of the Frankfurt Auschwitz trials between 1963 and 1965. Richter started to collect images taken from English and American photographers. These were included in the *Atlas* along with many other images from German magazines and his own photos. Richter juxtaposed the images of the camps with pornographic images. He eventually colored them over in garish colors. Richter initially intended to exhibit them in Düsseldorf but abandoned the project at the last minute. There are various interpretations of these efforts; the most compelling to me are those of Mark Godfrey, a British critic and curator at the Tate Modern, who argues that Richter was attempting to prevent the images from being inscribed in a monumentalist form.[14]

Richter's second attempt was occasioned by his being invited in 1997 to produce a design for the entry hall of the Reichstagsgebäude, the building where the German parliament, the Bundestag, meets in Berlin. The sketches of concentration camp inmates are preserved, once again in the *Atlas*, although Richter's ultimate submission does not include them. He originally thought of using images drawn from the camp photographs but abandoned the project. Richter substituted a vertical set of black, red, and yellow panels echoing the flag of the Weimar Republic. It is hard to imagine the Bundestag authorities approving the camp images in the entryway to the parliament building of the newly unified German Republic, but it must be said that they did approve a monumental construction commemorating the Holocaust, albeit a nonfigural one, across the street from the building.

Richter's third attempt was completed in 2014 (Richter was then eighty-two years old) and exhibited in Dresden. The works in the show were originally entitled *Abstract Paintings* and given a number in Richter's scrupulously managed *catalogue raisonné*. When the exhibition was moved to Baden-Baden in 2015, however, Richter changed the name to *Birkenau*. Birkenau was the largest of the six concentration camps where the Jewish genocide was carried out. It was built in 1940 and put into operation the following year. The Nazis began using the extermination system of gas chambers in the spring of 1942, and Birkenau was the last to cease their use in November 1944.

In a footnote to *Richters* Birkenau-*Bilder*, Buchloh observes that Richter changed the name of the exhibit after the influx of refugees from the Middle East and Africa, along with the rise of the far right in Germany, in particular in Dresden. This claim presumably would not have been made without at least tacit approval from Richter. That being said, it goes against the whole grain of Richter's lifelong eschewal of enabling ideological motives or interpretations of his work. Consequently, as of 2013–14 Richter remained in a liminal state about how to deal with this defining *kairos* of German history.[15]

For Richter, the awareness of a new possibility for image-making was cat-alyzed by his encounter with Georges Didi-Huberman's *Images malgré tout*. In a review of the book in a Frankfurt paper (11 February 2008), Richter dis-covered the existence of four clandestinely produced photographs taken (at great risk) from within the concentration camp by unidentified inmates or Jewish guards. At the time he came across the review, he put a copy of the images up on the wall of his studio but did not read the book. We will return to Didi-Huberman and his visit in December 2013 to Richter's studio later in this book.

Technē and *Pathosformel*

At first Richter considered a grisaille style parallel to the tones that he had used in *October 18, 1977,* the group of paintings he made of the deaths of the leaders of the Baader-Meinhof Red Army Faction in Stammheim prison. He worked on this style for over a year before abandoning it. He then produced four large abstract paintings that covered over traces of the representational forms.

Once he was satisfied with this work Richter digitally duplicated the paint-ings, thereby producing a second set of images, different in the technology of their production and by the fact of their division into four equal quad-rants: "The four equally sized canvasses were now covered with a netlike abstraction, an irregular grid structure, cohesive and coherent on all four surfaces; paintings whose chroma and facture one would have to describe as hesitant and confined rather than as articulating expressive gestures."[16] Richter exhibited the digital reproductions across from the paintings. The originals could not be sold (Richter will donate them to a museum), but the digital reproductions are available for purchase. For Buchloh, this strategy of duplication served to "subvert any false monumentality as well as dis-solving the fetishization of the singularized and spectactularized painterly object, intrinsically opposed to its mnemonic intentions."[17] Or as a gesture that "any commemorative approach to understanding the Shoah inevitably would have to expand its critical awareness to reflect on the catastrophes of the present and the imminent future as well."[18]

One can agree with the second claim, and I do, while not finding the first claim compelling.

It is uncontroversial but tautological to claim that Richter's painting is historically situated and/or that it is entangled with his autobiography. Today, it is also uncontroversial to maintain that there have been two regimes of denial of the atrocity of the Nazis in Germany: the Communist regime in the former East Germany and the West German postwar culture often characterized as infused with American consumerism.

Buchloh asserts that there has been an ethical imperative to consider these issues as articulated by a line of French and German philosophers. He cites passages from Karl Jaspers's 1946 essay on German guilt. Although he provides no evidence that Richter came to these questions through this literature, it is not controversial to claim that the topic was visible to all. More directly, Buchloh frames Adorno's famous 1949 challenge concerning the possibility or impossibility of art after Auschwitz. Buchloh's formulation is as follows: "Could post-bourgeois subjectivity have a concept after Auschwitz?"[19] Thus, his framing is epistemological, which he links to the formation or lack of formation of a subject position. This insistence on a theoretical framing of aesthetic issues is common among certain traditions of postwar art history and criticism and yet questionable, in my opinion, in its attribution of motives and beliefs to artists.

Buchloh writes that while still in East Germany, Richter understood that the times of avant-garde artists such as John Heartfield and Bertolt Brecht had come and gone.[20] Perhaps Richter concurred with this judgment, although as we shall see Richter admired what he refers to as bourgeois authors such as Thomas Mann while in the East and was surprised to find once he migrated to West Germany that he was supposed to despise them.

The four initial paintings were an answer in line with Adorno about the pornographic as culture after Auschwitz. The subsequent digital reproductions concerned the state and confronting the authorities with a memory of what had been. Although Richter did produce images that might have been considered to serve that purpose, the final project was far tamer with a color scheme reminiscent of the Weimar flag.

Regardless, there were other German artists roughly of Richter's generation, such as Joseph Beuys, who did make reflections on the knowledge of Auschwitz one of the foundations of their painterly projects. Richter kept a respectful distance from Beuys's performativity, his conceptions of nature, and his self-stylization. Yet, he never made this history central to his work in any explicit sense.

Buchloh offers two contrasting interpretations of Richter's self-understanding in 2013. The first: Richter was keenly aware that "the reception of his work in the present occurs precisely under the auspices of a total spectacularization and an economic speculation of artistic production."[21]

The first part of this claim seems wildly exaggerated and not something Richter could possible agree with: after all, he continues to paint ceaselessly and pays scrupulous attention to how his work is distributed. Richter has an excellent and up-to-date website that includes all of his painting as well as links to literature about him, list of current exhibitions, a repertoire of quotes, and so on. The second part no doubt does not escape his attention. Although Richter is generous in allowing his work to be reproduced for academic books and the like, he must be an extremely wealthy man, given the worldwide market for his paintings and their current market value. Buchloh attributes a form of guilty conscience or responsibility for Richter's return to attempts to artistically come to terms with the past crimes of Germany.

Kairos and Form and Casuistry II

Mark Godfrey, art critic and curator at the Tate where he was part of the team that curated the important retrospective of Richter's work, *Gerhard Richter: Panorama, a Retrospective, 2011*, had previously published a book strikingly relevant to these challenges in 2007, *Abstraction and the Holocaust*. Godfrey provides a contrastive—and to my mind a richer and more interesting as well as more accurate—interpretation of the solutions available for those seeking to make images in the wake of major catastrophic turning points in the history of the twentieth century. It is relevant that the major artists and architects Godfrey discusses (Morris Lewis, Frank Stella, Peter Eisenman, and others) all continued other work prior to and subsequent to their forays into the nettles of approaching image-making and the Nazis.

Godfrey underscores the range of possible artistic responses that have in fact been undertaken by numerous artists. It is true that the examples in his book concern non-German artists. Godfrey draws a helpful distinction when he writes: "There is a huge difference between an art historical one such as my own, which asks how specific artists have attempted to engage with the Holocaust at different moments, and a philosophical one, which considers how art should or should not respond to calamitous history."[22]

Although Godfrey did not write about Richter in the 2007 book, he became deeply familiar with Richter's working during the curatorial preparation of the Tate exhibit. He delivered a penetrating and insightful lecture at the conference accompanying the Tate exhibit's opening that deals directly with the thematic that Buchloh raises although adopting a different interpretation of how Richter has thematized them.

Although dealing with earlier material, Godfrey's proviso below applies, I think, trenchantly to Buchloh's interpretations. Godfrey writes:

> If the ideas of Adorno or Lyotard are mistreated, they could lend support to the kind of blanket claims about abstraction and its relationship to the Holocaust that I refuse. Abstraction could seem a vague condition of art after Auschwitz; a refusal to depict what cannot or should not be represented realistically; an art of respectful silence before sublime history.[23]

Godfrey is helpful in providing a discussion of what Adorno actually said (less sweeping than it has been taken to claim) as well as a caution about the whole vexed topic of the challenge of art and catastrophic turning points in history (which I am referring to as *kairoi*).

In 1949 Adorno concluded his essay *Cultural Criticism and Society* with what was to become a celebrated and debated maxim: "To write poetry after Auschwitz is barbaric." Adorno was not arguing that all artistic production was impossible after Auschwitz, as is often claimed, but rather that lyric poetry was impossible. That being said, Adorno was unquestionably asserting that all writing henceforth would take place within a frame of the historical trauma of the Nazis. Godfrey presents a modified but still powerful interpretation of Adorno's arguments, which is entirely apposite here. Godfrey takes Adorno to be saying: "To instrumentalize art is to undercut the opposition art mounts against instrumentalism."[24]

Framed in this manner, the issue is less one of possibility or impossibility but rather of ethos: how to take this imperative into account? This formulation generalizes the challenge while remaining within the purview of Adorno's historical setting and concerns. One might say, it is a step toward abstraction.

Concept: Differend

Godfrey introduces another step in reframing via Jean-François Lyotard's concept of the "differend" as conceptualizing the problem-space of those attempting to meet the challenge of art and catastrophe:

The event happened, but though the established discourses will not be able to articulate it, it must be witnessed. The "differend" is the name Lyotard gave to the state of representation for such an event: "The differend is the unstable state and instant of language wherein something which must be able to be put into phrases yet cannot be." "In the differend, something 'asks' to be put into phrases, and suffers from the wrong of not being able to be put into phrases right away." It was the task of art and philosophy to find differends and witness them: "What is at stake in a literature, in a philosophy, in a politics perhaps, is to bear witness to differends by finding idioms for them." The concept of the "differend" therefore conveys a sense of urgency (the event must be represented) and frustration (the event has destroyed the representational tools).[25]

Although the subject matter of this initial discussion is the Holocaust, I am arguing that the "differend" is not reducible to it alone but encompasses a wider field of existence and experience, specifically in the multiple events produced within the dynamic and unresolved motions of modernism and modernity.

Godfrey indicates not the impossibility of artistic production but rather the necessity at this point in history of a certain ethos. He writes: "I am arguing that at times, it was necessary and compelling for abstract artists to engage with history without jettisoning the language of their work—just as compelling as it was for other artists who felt instead that the only way to confront history was to reject abstraction."[26]

One can say that a broad problematization at a significant historical conjuncture makes multiple solutions available while foreclosing others. The foreclosure is not absolute and not given in advance in a determinative fashion.

Godfrey elaborates on Lyotard's understanding of the challenge of form under the sign of the differend. One determination, or foreclosure, with which Richter would concur in his own manner, is as follows: "Only that which has been inscribed can, in the current sense of the term, be forgotten."[27]

Stated most broadly the challenge is this: How could one bear witness to a differend through form-giving? Or how could an artistic production save memory without inscribing it in such a way that it will be forgotten?

OBJECT   The Contemporary

> Distance is not a safety zone but a field of tension. It is mani-
> fested not in relaxing the claim of ideas of truth, but in delicacy
> and fragility of thinking. . . . The distance of thought from reality
> is itself nothing but the precipitate of history in concepts.
> **—Theodor Adorno**

John Dewey, in his *Logic*, makes an informative distinction between things
and objects. Things are simply in the world. Objects are the products of inquiry. Dewey writes:

> The term *objects* will be reserved for the subject-matter so far as it has been
> produced and ordered in settled form by means of inquiry; proleptically, ob-
> jects are the *objectives* of inquiry. The apparent ambiguity of using "objects"
> for this purpose (since the word is regularly applied to things that are ob-
> served or thought of) is only apparent. For things exist *as* objects for us only
> as they have been previously determined as outcomes of inquiry. When used
> in carrying on new inquiries in new problematic situations, they are known
> as objects in virtue of prior inquiries that warrant their assertibility. In the
> new situation, they are *means* of attaining knowledge of something else. In
> the strict sense, they are part of the contents of inquiry. But retrospectively
> (that is, as products of prior determination in inquiry) they are objects.[1]

This somewhat idiosyncratic but perfectly coherent use of the term *object*
thus indicates that the term covers both the products of inquiry as well as
forming the objects, so to speak, of further inquiry.

Throughout this book I will follow a pattern of introducing Object sections. They will present to the reader the products of assembled syntheses that constitute the objects in virtue of prior inquiry and observation. They are the proverbial data. They are not a list of facts, although they are factual. They are not examples, although they are meant to be indicative, in a specific manner, of elements in a larger configuration. Thus, in my use, objects are a type of evidence. Being products of prior inquiry, it is fair to say, they are empirical. To that degree, they can be used to diagnose and define with more clarity the parameters of a subsequent stage of inquiry.

Objects and Objectives 1: The Contemporary

The first such object concerns *the contemporary*. Furthering an understanding of this object, how it might best be approached and to what end, constitutes a central objective of my efforts.

The venerable avant-garde journal *October* devoted a large portion of its Fall 2009 issue, number 131, to "A Questionnaire on the Contemporary." Hal Foster, writing on behalf of the journal's editors, sent out the following questionnaire to seventy critics and curators. He notes that very few curators responded. The questionnaire reads as follows:

> The category of "contemporary art" is not a new one. What is new is the sense that, in its very heterogeneity, much present practice seems to float free of historical determination, conceptual definition, and critical judgment. Such paradigms as "the neo-avant-garde" and "postmodernism" which once oriented some art and theory, have run into the sand, and arguably, no models of much explanatory reach or intellectual force have risen in their stead. At the same time, perhaps paradoxically, "contemporary art" has become an institutional object in its own right: in the academic world there are professorships and programs, and in the museum world departments and institutions, all devoted to the subject, and most tend to treat it as apart not only from prewar practice but from most postwar practice as well.
>
> Is this floating-free real or imagined? A merely local perception? A simple effect of the end-of-grand narratives? If it is real, how can we specify some of its principal causes, that is, beyond general reference to "the market" and "globalization"? Or is it indeed a direct outcome of a neolib-

eral economy, one that, moreover, is now in crisis? What are some of its salient consequences for artists, critics, curators, and historians—for their formation and their practice alike? Are there collateral effects in other fields of art history? Are there instructive analogies to be drawn from the situation in other arts and disciplines? Finally, are there benefits to this apparent lightness of being?[2]

1a. Consensus

All of the responses—thirty-two out of the seventy invited—are conspicuously staid. Although the majority of the respondents are cutting-edge academic critics (most of them employed in the elite institutions of the American university system), in their responses none take any stylistic liberties of any significance and none experiment with form. It is as if they had been sent a questionnaire, which they took literally in the way that deep down they knew was what they excelled at doing: writing academic prose and agilely performing in situating themselves as cutting-edge. The tone, and the undertones, of disquiet of the replies reveals that there are felt to be vital stakes involved in the issues raised; the reason perhaps for the gravity of the responses rides as well on the fact that how to answer these questions both within the critical university establishment and in the art world of museums, galleries, auction houses, and festivals remains unsettled. In fact, the negotiated distance or lack thereof between these diverse fields of symbolic and monetary capital, to use Pierre Bourdieu's terms, is a principal stake, a source of anxiety, and a fountainhead of uncertainty for those concerned.

Although there are nuances of tone, of insight, and of fervor to be found in the range of responses, almost all of them insightful, a consistent broad thematic does run across the replies; few, if any, contest *October*'s tentative diagnosis of the state of things in the world of art and art criticism. Significantly, none of the respondents actually directly takes up Hal Foster's challenge to move beyond "general references to the 'market' and 'globalization.'" This lack of engagement does not mean that "globalization" or the "market" are not being constantly invoked and evoked, only that no sustained, serious sociological or economic analysis is provided (or even referenced). This absence of scholarly curiosity, or felt necessity, to engage a vast literature on these topics is striking and revelatory: this is a self-referential peer group that has internalized the existing genre constraints at work in their disciplines. Or perhaps, these critics are so dependent and connected to the turbulent effects of these myriad market forces and the venues and trends they create that to take the time to address them in an adequate manner would be to exclude oneself from the current hyper-accelerated game of contemporary art. Time is of the essence, and timeliness is mandatory. Apparently, being untimely is too risky professionally at this conjuncture for these contemporaries.

There is broad agreement that even though there is no stable scholarly or commercial consensus on what contemporary art is (and is not), the growth over the course of the last two decades of the twentieth century of institutions to display it, explore it, and sell it has been rapid and defining. Not only has there been an expansion of the scale of the well-known biennales; there has also been a globalization of their sites and contributors as more and more venues are created, financed, and visited by artists, dealers, curators, and critics as well as tourists and amateurs of all kinds. More surprisingly, given the dispositional and institutional lethargy of the academic world, there has been a mushroom-like establishment of university investment in contemporary or contemporary/modern art with the associated courses at both the graduate and undergraduate levels. And, of course, there has been a "transience" in the branding of the object being named (if such it be) driven by a great flow of money, or artistic producers and directors, of critics within and outside of museums, auction houses, and the academy. And then, lest we forget, there is the Internet.

It would almost certainly be misleading, however, to characterize the state of affairs in this part of the art world as a crisis. To call it a crisis would imply that the existence of the older art institutions is in danger; that suddenly there was a steep falling-off of money and audience (as in the classical music world); or that the mood of those involved was either somber or torpid. As none of these conditions apply, we can only say that "the times they are a-changin'."

Thus, for an anthropologist of the contemporary, the art world's contemporary qualifies as a plausible object of study and reflection. As an undertaking, such a study is neither my current goal nor consonant with my expertise. Here I offer a few observations in order to get clearer about the current range of the term "the contemporary"—and to clear some more ground for subsequent explorations.

1b. Accelerations: The View from MoMA's Escalator

One of a small number of curators to respond to *October*'s questionnaire was Helen Molesworth—head of the Department of Modern and Contemporary Art (created in 1997) and the Houghton Curator of Contemporary Art at the Harvard Art Museum. Her reflections are among the most thoughtful and balanced of those appearing in the issue. Her core diagnosis of the current state of play turns in part on her observation that "for many, the unanswerability of questions about quality, the lack of consensus about importance, the newfound vitality of the viewer, and the perpetual influx of new art are all causes to rejoice."[3] As a curator, Molesworth cannot comfortably embrace this state of affairs, which she nicely labels "festivalism." The reason for her discursive pitch of caution is that, as a curator, she is obliged, after all is said and done, to make choices precisely about quality, importance, vitality, and the cacophonous influx of artistic production. She laments the fact that even her most distinguished fellow curators, even while they are organizing shows at the most prestigious and well-funded institutions on contemporary art, are uncharacteristically unsure and noncommittal; after some hesitation, they have decided to make a virtue of what they take to be a necessity. She writes tellingly that even "MoMA [the Museum of Modern Art in New York] seems unwilling to narrativize what is at stake."[4] And that refusal authorizes others in less prestigious institutions not to commit to a standard beyond the numbers of people drawn to visit the museum or gallery, the experience of the art and artists, and a sense that another show will soon be on exhibit.

Johanna Burton—associate director and senior faculty member of the Whitney Museum Independent Study Program in New York City—describes her disquiet and irritation while riding the escalators at MoMA at the cascade of things on display apparently without order or hierarchy except, of course, that they are at MoMA and hence are valuable and worthy of regard, however obligatorily nonjudgmental. One might say that she regrets being mandated to occupy the stance of a *flâneur* when she was trained to be an arbiter of taste. The contemporary operates as a category, Burton writes, in two different ways: "as a category so pluralist and wide-reaching in its vicissitudes and effects that it would seem all-encompassing, *and* as a newly secured 'institutional object' recognized as particular (or at least pervasive) enough to be jockeying for legitimacy within the field of art history."[5] The theme of the dispersion of authority is introduced by a number of respondents with notable ambivalence. Alexander Alberro, the Virginia Bloedel Wright Associate Professor of Art History at Barnard College and Columbia University, observes: "Gone is the chic collector who seeks cultural capital, let alone the connoisseur of early modernism; art collecting today is largely dominated by purchase of sheer speculation."[6]

This diagnosis is linked to a broader claim that there is a near total void of a sophisticated and conceptually rich analysis of reception. What is mentioned, perhaps a little timidly and sotto voce, by a number of these art historians, is the felt need to reestablish, in some fashion or other, that fashion being undersigned and undefended, the learned critic's privilege and legitimate authority to lay claim to judgments of "objectivity" and "disinterestedness." Of course, theory-driven critical discourse within the elite academy over the last several decades has itself spearheaded the deconstruction of such notions as merely historical, arbitrary remnants of modernism and its advocates. Additionally, the blurring or elimination of the line between high and low, or popular and elite, or individual and community, or art production and art criticism has been established with a near hegemonic authority. Some of those who championed these developments, and who still, to an extent at least, appreciate their value, are now wondering about some of the unexpected ramifications of their theorizing practice.

> Current artistic practice is extremely heterogeneous, yet in theoretical and critical writing on contemporary art one often finds a quite consistent set of terms employed to analyze artistic practices. I am thinking in particular of Agamben's "homo sacer," "bare life," and "state of exception"; Jean-Luc Nancy's "inoperative community"; Jacques Rancière's "partition of the sensible"; Negri and Hardt's "multitude"; Laclau and Mouffe's "radical democracy"; and Balibar's "transnational citizenship."[7]

It seems at times as if awareness was suddenly stirring among these holders of endowed chairs that they are reaping what they, or their advisers, have sown. Among those ramifications appears a current that negates or eludes the very practice of history as the study of a past per se:

Perhaps paradoxically, then, the horizon of contemporary art history is in fact the past, not the present. The field against or on which it operates is what we think we already know. The present is not arrived at through the past but the reverse. I think contemporary art history is best when it is de/constructivist of "contemporary," "art" and "history" alike.[8]

The only paradox is that one stream of *doxa* has become dominant. And that dominance increasingly precludes, at least in certain venues, a sustained attention to and presentation of the past. The line between "presentism" and the "history of the present" is, when it comes down to it, underconceptualized and no longer controlled by those who are, or were, authorized to think about such arcane topics.

1c. The Beautiful Cloud

Although MoMA's curators are apparently reluctant to name the order obtaining in the contemporary art scene, others are not so reluctant: one offering of the contemporary state of affairs has been "narrativized" in Yves Michaud's short book (or long essay) *L'art à l'état gazeux: Essai sur le triomphe de l'esthétique* published in the summer of 2003.[9] Michaud, a prolific philosopher and critic in the Parisian style, argues that the special domain of art as the privileged site of the aesthetic, which had prevailed for centuries, has come to an end. What has replaced it, gradually for a time, and then in an accelerated and triumphant fashion more recently, is the ever-increasing spread—like a cloud of invisible and euphoria-inducing gas—of the aesthetic into more and more realms of life.

Michaud identifies three main causes for the state of the contemporary situation. The first is the progressive undermining and eventual disappearance of the art object as the unchallenged pivot of the aesthetic experience. Michaud provides a long discussion of the gradual dissolution of the autonomous art object during the progressive triumph of modern art over the course of the twentieth century. He traces genealogically the origin of this dissolution in modernism to the decade of the 1910s with the appearance and eventual acceptance of collage (papier collé). Sixty years later, he cites the critic and advocate of modernism, Harold Rosenberg, as having identified as early as 1972 the de-aestheticization of the art object. These and a plethora of other examples bolster Michaud's thesis that the end of the autonomous art object does not by any means entail the end of art: quite the opposite in Michaud's view.

As the art object became displaced and eventually replaced by a broader understanding and practice of the aesthetic experience, it became clear quite early on in the process that there could be multiple other paths leading to such an experience than painting and the other nineteenth-century fine arts. If it is the "effect" side that begins to colonize aesthetic experience, then the trend to more and more technical means of generating such experiences is not surprising. It follows that its production requires engineers and managers as much as artists. The twentieth century has seen a vast expansion of the industrial production of cultural and symbolic goods. Perhaps most famously in the Bauhaus, the older demarcation zones were brought into closer proximity. This process certainly had its democratizing dimension; it also required more standardization and the industries that could make such products available for mass distribution.[10]

The Bauhaus is emblematic of the adjacency and collaborative efforts to bring art, craft, standardization, pedagogy, and industry into apparatuses designed to reshape daily life in an industrial economy and society. Less obviously instrumental were Marcel Duchamp's readymades; they became emblematic, Michaud argues convincingly, of how an artist's gesture transferred the vast world and an ever-expanding world of ordinary objects into the field of artistic or aesthetic gravity. Once Duchamp made a urinal a museum piece, the arrow between art and daily life began to run back and forth in tandem, transforming the precious status of both as well as the boundaries that had obtained between them. Michaud captures one aspect of this motion nicely when he says: "Art has spread; the children and grandchildren of Duchamp have filled the world with ready-mades."[11] The generalization of this process of delocalization, production, and relocalization—former art objects sent on their way into the world of daily use by the Bauhaus and industrial objects fabricated in principle for their utility or prestige sent into museums and galleries as aesthetic objects—has proved to be expansive.

Michaud argues that this process and its associated experiences continue to be more and more pervasive. With the kind of dissolution and disassociation occasioning such anxiety among our contemporary art critics and curators, all is not lost. Today there are no fixed and a priori boundaries: "Nonetheless what remains is the fact that all sorts of practices, *absolutely all*, can at any moment and under certain conditions become part of contemporary art."[12] Once the object domain became a museum without walls and the walls of the museum became a space for objects without limits, the next step in Michaud's narrative is that the experience of these objects and the experience of that experience were opened up for aestheticization in a definitive fashion. John Dewey's pragmatist advocacy of "Art as Experience" has come to fruition, albeit hardly in the form that Dewey imagined. Things ramify.

1d. Decelerations: A Different Contemporary

Enter, once again, contemporary art. Johanna Burton of the Whitney provides a claim I can almost agree with. She writes:

> When Roland Barthes asked in 1971, "Is not to be modern to know clearly what cannot be started over again?," he was suggesting that sometimes so-called critical distance draws a very firm line between past and present — too firm as Barthes saw it. [. . .] What the contemporary offers — when it is allowed to operate as a way of thinking broadly about the conditions for artistic production and reception we are ourselves experiencing — is the opportunity for praxis. Writing, thinking, and teaching about art whose consequences we cannot fully know provides us a kind of meta-exercise, one not dissociated from historical accounts but, rather, alive and awake to connections to be made between now and then while nonetheless aware of their utter incompatibilities.[13]

Why "utter incompatibilities"? Had she omitted "utter," then the link to practice and reflection would seem plausible, contemporary in a different, and to my mind better, sense. If the line between past and present is so firm as to be utterly impassable, then we are, it seems to me, once again, into a form of modernism, or perhaps without a faith and seriousness of a movement, simply postmodernism.

Contemporary Art and Criticism

There are moments in life when the question of knowing if one could think differently than how one thinks and perceive differently than how one sees is indispensable for continuing to observe and reflect.
—Michel Foucault

Charles Baudelaire, Foucault's emblematic modern critic, was confident that he knew what the best modern painting was; he devoted much of his time to the métier of art critic.[14] Nietzsche also devoted himself to aesthetic criticism, especially of music, as his recurrent and frequent attention to Wagner demonstrates. His notebooks are filled with attempts to figure out what the music of his time should be and whether or not Wagner was the person who was leading the way forward. Nietzsche, of course, for a time accompanied Wagner, literally at Bayreuth, and then feeling betrayed, left him behind with a storm of vituperation.

Lest this reference to Wagner seem merely anecdotal, Foucault's trips to Bayreuth with Pierre Boulez (and other friends) and his reflections on the director Patrick Chéreau's staging of Wagner's *Ring* cycle would indicate otherwise.[15] In a long article Foucault wrote for the Italian newspaper *Corriere della Sera*, reviewing the performance of the cycle in Bayreuth in 1980, he provides a beautiful, acid-seared aesthetic of the contemporary.[16]

Boulez, Chéreau, and the set designer Peduzzi were confronted with the question: what to do with Wagner today? The question was inevitable, and no doubt its daunting magnitude is what drew these stellar and highly different artists to accept that challenge. Foucault briefly rehearses the core answers that had been given to that inevitable question. There had been an attempt to avoid the history of the last century and its nefarious associations so as to get back to something in the music, staging, and power of the *Ring* that continued to make it worthy and compelling for so many; pure mythology was one solution but that meant focusing on Wagner's mythology, which was, for Foucault, both "explosive and derisory." After the Second World War, the solutions varied between attempted historical solutions (setting the scene in one past or another, one pre-Nazi in East Germany, another with a full awareness of the awful political legacy in the West). Chéreau and Peduzzi also avoided staging the musical drama as a kind of assemblage in the manner of Bertolt Brecht, which would have entailed making the differences between chronological references apparent and inassimilable: the epoch to which the Ring explicitly refers; the time in which it was written; the present moment during which it was being performed.[17]

It was in the crossroads that Boulez and company took up the challenge in 1976. Boulez was at first sight an unlikely choice for conductor. He was, after all, one of the great formalist innovators in twentieth-century music, known for his difficult avant-garde pieces and vast erudition. To have an arch exemplar of modernism interpret Wagner's scores for the cycle—so filled with the noise, fury, and images of nineteenth-century mythologizing—was, to say the least, hazardous for both the festival and the conductor. The first performance was very poorly received by the Wagner faithful at Bayreuth; it was greeted with hisses and boos. Five years of annual performances, however, gradually familiarized these faithful to what Boulez was attempting to do. In 1980, when Foucault witnessed the performance, the applause at the end of the performance lasted an hour and a half, resulting in over one hundred curtain calls.

What had Boulez done? His solution—to cut to the chase—can only be described as providing a *contemporary* solution. It was, Foucault argues, precisely Boulez's depth of knowledge and loyalty to the musical changes of the twentieth century that allowed him to find and give form to a living "meaning to musical drama," neither opera, music, or drama alone. What was that meaning? Among the early criticism of Boulez and company's staging and arrangement was the charge that he had merely *accompanied* the drama with Wagner's music. Although Foucault agreed that that is what Boulez had done, he posed the critical issue: "But one must understand what kind of accompaniment it is a question of."[18]

And Foucault provides the elements of how Boulez chose to accompany the work of Chéreau, Peduzzi, and Wagner:

Boulez took seriously the Wagnerian idea of a drama in which music and text do not repeat each other, are not saying each in its own way the same thing; but rather one in which the orchestra, the song, the play of the actors, the tempos of the music, the movements of the scene, the decors must be composed as partial elements so as to constitute, during the time of the performance, a unique form, a singular event.[19]

Through this rigorous adherence to listening to and not forgetting the series of developments in contemporary music from Wagner to us, Wagner has become "one of our own" (une part de la nôtre).[20]

Gerhard Richter's Assemblages

One of the distinctive and striking aspects of Gerhard Richter's production is the amount of prose that he has produced, singularly or in multiple interviews, and publications. This production is striking because Richter himself seems somewhat shy in person and is not especially articulate. Furthermore, he often demurs from the interviewer's interpretations of his work. One might suppose that these interviews and exchanges of letters and the like are simply a means for Richter to be social, to clarify his thoughts, to respond to critics and the like. It is probably the case that all of the above apply. The question remains: why publish all of this material?

One simple reason is that Richter is a man of order. As is evident in his cataloguing of his prodigious production, the periodic updating of his *catalogue raisonnée* with inclusions and exclusions, Richter keeps track of things. But why make this public? One reason is that it facilitates the sale of his work; by this point in his life Gerhard Richter must be an extremely rich man. A recent auction sold one of his abstract paintings for the highest price ever received by a living artist.[21] Richter is a bourgeois, living in a spacious compound of house and studio, presumably supporting his current and past wives and his children. For a long time now he has employed assistants in the studio as well as a business staff, glimpses of whom can be seen in the film *Gerhard Richter Painting.* He has an archivist.

Perhaps most striking of all, he is quite open about this. Although he appears (or presents himself) as modest and unpretentious, open to encounters and public appearances, not to mention a continuous flow of exhibitions that he supervises and attends, he has not objected to being called with some regularity "the most important living artist."[22]

Paradoxically enough, perhaps this unabashed embodiment of high bourgeois lifestyle with its celebration of domesticity and the like is one of his most iconoclastic features. Just as Richter asserts that there is no reason why he cannot return to and learn from German Romantic painting without being a German Romantic painter, so, too, he is breaking the mold of the modern painter, the anti-bourgeois, bohemian, often mysterious and/ or self-destructive artist.

For example, in a publication entitled "Notes 1989" (14 March) Richter writes:

> The word "bourgeois," formerly a compliment, now negative in its connotations, much used, always vaguely polemical, jejune and irrelevant. "Bourgeois" equals tidy, educated, law-abiding, in contrast to flipped-out, cheerfully dressed, ostentatiously nonconformist (e.g., Thomas Mann as against Bertolt Brecht, President Weizsäcker as against Joschka Fischer).
>
> Just as conformism is not at all the same thing as security—the word denotes a deference to prevailing fashions, and to the prevailing climate or system, which springs from stupidity, cowardice, indolence and baseness—nonconformism is not necessarily its diametrical opposite, but often springs from a courage born of stupidity and blindness. Nonconformist laxity often originates in the confined, retarded structure of mindless insolence.[23]

There is, however, a pronounced restiveness. Richter is self-critical and self-aware. He has developed an insistent technē of working, reworking, observing, revisiting, and at times destroying his paintings. Although there is nothing unusual about that per se, Richter while encouraging response and informed criticism rarely seems to overtly agree with it. His self-characterization of how he knows whether a painting is finished or good is cryptic. His assistants (who appear in the film) make equally hesitant evaluations of how Richter decides something is done. They remark that he returns to paintings he had expressed admiration for and at times redoes them, or the opposite, returning to work he is not satisfied with and finding a means to remediate it.

Therefore, when Richter does respond to criticism, it is worth paying attention to what irked him. In his "Letter to Walter Grasskamp on the Subject of *18 October 1977*," dated 17 October 1989, Richter responds in part:

> I could just dismiss all of this as helpless rubbish, but the painful thing about it is that you entangle your thinking in strategic categories, that you accuse me of your own purely tactical political sense, and in doing so you undermine any attempt I could make to clarify to you my actual motiva-

tions. Following this train of thought it's only natural that you come to the determination that the death of the RAF [Rote Armee Fraktion] members I was interested in can only be seen as the "expression of a political — and therefore quite abstract" — failure. It seems apparent, though, there is something "quite abstract" about you, particularly when I see now your discomfort with "covert radicalism." I must tell you that I have never strived for radicalism (something I have stated publicly on several occasions) because as a matter of fact I have other concerns. In the same way, the question of whether I am making history paintings or not could hardly be less important to me.

However, I consider not quite so unimportant your false accusation that the paintings allow the viewer "to read into them anything he wants" — because even if you saw the paintings as nothing more than a catalogue of reproductions, surely you would have imagined a huge list of everything that was not visible in them.

And then at the same time you do find a way to claim something is lacking: for example, in the case of Hanns Martin Schleyer: "the photos of his disintegration as a hostage" and "the ghostly shots of the crime scene with the corpse of the driver and the bodyguards." Sure, that sounds really striking, but it is a patently malicious misrepresentation of the theme of my work, which you go on to accuse me of making it "seem as if the government had driven" the terrorists "to their death." Don't even you yourself think that's a bit mean?

And at the end of all this you are "taken aback." Suspicion arises in you because certain photos of individuals were not allowed to be reproduced (for the protection of family members) and because I did not wish to have the paintings sold on the art market.

I can only view these suspicions as abject and cynical; and, in comparison, all your other misrepresentations become irrelevant — even the hair-raising nonsense that I paint solely "pictures of pictures," and never of reality. This is nothing more than appalling high school art theory.

Perhaps you'll notice that in taking issue here, if ever so briefly, I've actually grappled with your article; while for your part, instead of criticizing the paintings, you merely speculated about motivations and imputed strategies, thus denouncing the work.[24]

On the one hand, this exchange (or the part of it we have) can readily be seen as an example of why the bourgeois/nonconformist binary is so dated. It is deployed here against Richter as a polemic that pigeonholes everything he has done to "appalling high school art theory." On the other hand, and of more interest, is the fact that Richter had been attacked on both the right and the left with polemic assaults marked by their utter assurance of the intent and meanings of the paintings. Ultimately, Richter sold the paintings to the Museum of Modern Art in New York rather than the museums in Frankfurt (where these events had taken place). This act equally aroused indignation.

The two charges that Richter angrily answers in the letter quoted above are that anyone can read anything into his paintings and that he does not paint reality. Richter seems aroused to self-justification although he only offers a bare minimum (that he did not want to put other families in danger, etc.). To arrive at a full vindicatory position, one might expect, would have required a ringing and elaborate explanation of how to see the paintings. And while it is true that in other interviews Richter does provide aspects of such instructions and explanations, perhaps the basic act of vindication (in the double sense of the term) was his act to sell the paintings to MoMA. Let them be seen as paintings (the Americans after all were not familiar with the details of Hanns Martin Schleyer's kidnapping and murder by the Red Army Faction [Rote Armee Fraktion] when it happened in 1977 and certainly not decades later). Perhaps by so doing, Richter joined a long and distinguished list of Germans who exiled themselves, for a time, to the United States (Thomas Mann, Bertolt Brecht, and Theodor Adorno, among others).

Reproaches: Counter-effectuations

In an incandescent footnote (which he did not read to his audience) during a lecture he did not intend for publication in the form it was presented, Michel Foucault advocated adopting "a very firm attitude" when faced with reproaches from critics. Certain objections, to use our vocabulary, are constituted as traps luring the sincere or fearful into a maze of double binds. Foucault's counsel, learned from years of experience in the strife-riven discursive fields of Paris: One must desist from defending oneself against a range of insidious reproaches since "in defending oneself from them one inevitably subscribes to what they maintain."[25]

Foucault proposed three types of possible counter-effectuations to the most common reproaches one was likely to encounter at the time (and still today). The following section consists of quotes from Foucault's footnote rearranged to suit this situation. The standard attacks (either implicitly or explicitly) demand adherence to theory, universals and/or systems of values.

To objections that postulate the disqualification of nihilism/nominalism/ historicism, we should try to reply by undertaking a historicist, nominalist, and nihilist analysis of this current. By this I mean: not construct this form of thought in its universal systematic character and justify it in terms of truth or moral value, but rather seek to know how the constitution and development of this critical game, this form of thought, was possible.

The question of historicism is: what have been and may be the effects of historical analysis in the field of historical thought?
A historicizing negativism, since it involves replacing a theory of knowledge, power, or the subject with the analysis of historically determinate practices.

A nominalist negativism, since it involves the replacing of universals like madness, crime, and sexuality with the analysis of experiences that constitute singular historical forms.
The question of nominalism is: what have been the effects of nominalist criticism in the analysis of cultures, knowledge, institutions, and political structures?

A negativism with a nihilistic tendency, if by this we understand a form of reflection which, instead of indexing practices to systems of values which allow them to be assessed, inserts these systems of values in the interplay of arbitrary but intelligible practices.
The question of nihilism is: what have been and what may be the effects of nihilism in the acceptance and transformation of systems of values?[26]

A doubt lingers: in what mode should one cast these counter-effectuations? One might well cast them ironically or heroically. Foucault more often than not preferred the latter. Admirable. Modern.

Beyond Reproach

Richter is no hermit or artistic purist above the fray. As I have noted, his writings and practices have been complexly engaged with a range of critics of multiple kinds. What follows is an exchange between Richter and Benjamin Buchloh, who is currently a professor of modern art at Harvard.

BB: Why have you so firmly rejected any concrete political intention in your art?

GR: Because politics does not suit me, because art has an entirely different function, because all I can do is paint. Call it conservative.

BB: But by limiting yourself to the medium of painting might not you be espousing not just a conservative position but maybe also a critical dimension? Are you, for instance, calling into question the immediacy claimed by work like that of Beuys?

GR: Naturally, by limiting myself to painting I imply a criticism of a lot of things that I don't like, not all of them connected with painting.

BB: So you don't deny on principle that someone might validly intend to make a critical political statement through art?

GR: I probably do deny it. But what counts is that I have to ask as my starting point, my foundation, my own possibilities, and my own premises.[27]

From another interview with Buchloh in 2004, we include the following snippets.[28]

BB: So, you are the last great painter?

GR: When you put it that way, I don't know how else to answer.

BB: Do you believe that painting is really about the preservation of masterful, individualist, artisanal production? Or don't you much rather think that it's about the conceptual, cognitive and perceptual foundations of the work of art, which can be saved in paintings?

GR: It all fits together, though.

BB: Well, isn't it what you want to preserve there this extreme ambiguity of your work, a contradictoriness unimaginable for anyone else, which really can only be produced by painterly means?

GR: No, it could be produced by other means as well. For my "Panes of Glass," the same criteria apply as I use in judging a painting by Chardin.

BB: What about when, in the present moment, you paint the structure of silicate?

GR: In the end it doesn't matter what I paint, it is always about the same quality.

BB: So, it's more about a specific definition of the differentiated subjectivity, not specific techniques that need to be rescued?

GR: I would never want to rescue a technique.

BB: What makes you so confident?

GR: . . . even the present has moments of promise . . .

2

CONSTELLATIONS   Writing and Imaging Strife

> I think he [Richter] has succeeded in creating a memorial against terrorism, against ideological fanaticism.
> —**Hubertus Butin**

My working hypothesis is that the problem-space of how to render strife visible (and enunciable) operates differently in a contemporary mode than it did in a modern one. Today, it appears that *uncertainty* is a more trenchant variable than is *determination*, that *restive recalcitrance* better captures the modes of subjectivation than does *ironic heroism*, and so on.[1]

Streit: Strife Not Struggle

As a device to approach the topic of strife, I employ two German terms: *Streitschrift* and *Streit-Bild*. Terms, Richard McKeon taught us at the University of Chicago, are composed of words + concepts + referents. It follows that a current challenge is to delineate and reflect on a preliminary analysis of candidate concepts and referents.

Why translate the German word *Streit* as "strife" and not "struggle"? Although there are a range of reasons for this decision, the main one here is that it helps to draw attention to the different concepts and referents engaged by one word or the other. Thus, the word and the term *struggle* have been used for two centuries now predominantly either as a political concept or as a psychological one or as the mutual interrelations of these two registers. Today, it seems to me that *struggle* has become a tired trope, ultimately a term whose current usage contributes to the ongoing withering of its potency. Attempting to remediate the term *struggle* would entail breaking down the term into its component parts—replacing the older concept and referents, modifying them, or at least defending them in innovative ways given their history and changed current conditions. That work would likely constitute a fruitless task given (among other things) the affective fields in which the term arose and has long since been historically integrated.

Contrastively, an advantage of the topic *strife* is that it disrupts the taken-for-granted modernist semantics. By doing so, it brings to light the need for careful inspection of the components of this and other such common topics and terms, thereby opening up the space for reconsideration and possible remediation. Said differently, such disruption makes it possible to identify instances in which other terms and relations can be seen more clearly themselves to be at issue.

Thus, it is plausible to maintain that *struggle* arose, cohered, and was taken for granted within an ethos of modernity, given that ethos's heroic mode of subjectivation (individual or collective) as well as its prior status as a key principle within philosophies of history during the nineteenth and twentieth centuries. The term's very conditions of success are arguably now its conditions of waning. This claim does not exclude the possibility that situations best characterized as struggle can continue to occur. To establish a state of affairs as an instance, example, or case of struggle, however, requires intellectual labor, not gestures of self-evidence. It is a working hypothesis here that such labor into the current practices and discursive uses of *struggle* would benefit from focusing first on an analysis of its relationship internal to the force/power couplet rather than one that began by linking struggle immediately to politics.

Sōzein (Care, Protection, Maintenance, Doing Good)

Strife used as a topic opens the opportunity to explore its linkages with other topics. One such category (encompassing terms and topics) is *sōzein*. Linking strife to *sōzein* might well open a path to discovering a range of considerations and practices embedded within situations taken up as ones of strife. Michel Foucault has directed our attention to this archaic term in his 1981–82 lectures at the Collège de France:

In Greek, the verb *sōzein* (to save) or the substantive *sōteria* (salvation) have a number of common meanings. *Sōzein* (to save) is (1) first of all to save from a threatening danger. One will say, for example, to save from a shipwreck, from a defeat, or to save from an illness. *Sōzein* also means (2) (a second major field of signification) to guard, protect, or keep a protective shield around something so that it can remain in its existing condition. [. . .] Third, (3) in a similar but clearly more moral sense, *sōzein* means to preserve and protect something like decency, honor or perhaps memory. [. . .] Fourth signification: (4) the juridical meaning. For a lawyer (or for someone who speaks on behalf of someone else), for example, to save (someone) is obviously to help him escape an accusation leveled against him. At the same time, it is to exonerate him. It is to preserve his innocence. Fifth, (5) *sōzesthai* (the passive form) means to be safe at the moment, that is to say, to remain, kept in the same condition as one was in previously. [. . .] A town will be saved, *sothēnai*, survive and be preserved if it does not relax its laws. So, if you like, there is the idea of maintenance in the former condition, in the primitive or original state of purity. Finally, and sixthly, (6) *sōzein* has an even more positive sense. *Sōzein* means to do good. It means to ensure the well-being, the good condition of something, someone or of a collectivity.[2]

The use of the couple strife/*sōzein* calls for a diagnostic response: what type and intensity of strife is at hand? What kind of care and protection are available or can be invented? The range and scale of care, repair, and protection is highly variable and remains to be explored. Ultimately, as an element in a contemporary ethos, *strife* might well enable a replacement or modification of relations assumed to be antagonistic ones with an understanding that takes them up as agonistic ones. Conversely, relations taken to be harmonious might well open up unrecognized dynamics of strife and/or practices of care and protection. It remains to be defined in this domain (as opposed, for example, to synthetic biology and bio-ethics) how the situations of discordance and indetermination arise, are understood, and remediated (when that happens).

Lament

In the ever-expanding, almost uniquely art-historical, secondary literature on Gerhard Richter, critics have focused the core of their historiographical and critical attention on Richter's technique of blurring worked-over photographic images, his family paintings that they take up as nostalgic domestic throwbacks, or troubling portrayals of his family's Nazi past, the ambiguous status of Richter's vast production of so-called abstract images, and the meaning of his frequent change of medium.

In the last several decades, attention centered on the significance of his *October 18, 1977* group with its series of painted images of the deaths of members of the Red Army Faction.[3] Most recently, as archives become available, work is ongoing on the GDR archives and other materials previously unavailable for scrutiny, especially the young artist's training and outlook in artistic technique and form. In sum, on the one hand, the critical literature has mainly concentrated on Richter's diverse techniques, and, on the other hand, a smaller body of commentary has taken up the artist's work and life in representational terms, addressing what they interpret as the content and significance of Richter's image-work and the reasons for the inclusion of that content and its underlying and unifying significance.[4]

As to the ratio of praise to blame, whether tacit or explicit, art critics and cultural commentators have sustained almost without exception a cautious and tentative approach rather than a judgmental one: what exactly is Richter doing in this or that canvas, this or that series? It is only occasionally, and often not without hesitancy, whose tone expresses a sense that one might be missing the point, that critics offer explicit judgments as to either the quality or the meaning of an instance of Richter's work. Thus, sustainable judgments as to whether Richter and his work are good or bad, successful or unsuccessful, meaningful or not, politically right wing or left wing are sparse. There are occasional explicit bits of praise (like the one in the epigraph above), but these are more throwaway lines than sustained evaluations.

Throughout his career, Richter has made himself widely available to critics and commentators; this affable availability as well as the quality and range of Richter's work seems to have kept many critics off-guard and simply hesitant to make nuanced evaluations of his prodigious output. Given how habitually uninhibited in its judgments the art-critical world is, and given the attachments to high theory in the academy with its historical and political perspectives, as well as the value-laden global art market, whatever Richter's techniques are for escaping more skeptical and sustained scrutiny should be marked by cultural observers as worthy of more attention.

Granted, Richter has neither endorsed nor elaborated specific criteria to identify success or failure in his work. For example, in the film *Gerhard Richter Painting*, we see several scenes of Richter pondering his freshly painted canvases, acknowledging to the off-screen questioner that he is not yet sure whether they are done or not, are successful or not, or they please him or not. In the film, Richter's assistants attest to the fact that he not infrequently changes his mind about the status and quality of a painting over the course of short intervals (days, weeks)—at times leaving a canvas untouched after initially expressing uncertainty, hesitation, or even approval about its status; at other times entirely painting over a canvas; or at yet other times making either minor alterations or else major squeegee and/or color alterations to either parts or to the canvas as a whole. Only the master knows for sure, and he is not always so sure—and certainly is not saying.

The exception that proves the rule are the interpretations of Richter given by Kaja Silverman, whose psychoanalytic and feminist readings, although provocative as well as contestable, seem to have elicited little published response from other critics. For example, the claims and interpretive criteria put forth at her keynote presentation at the Tate symposium at the opening of the *Panorama* exhibit stood in stark opposition to a number of other presentations. Silverman's central interpretive strategy has been to analyze Richter as working through unresolved psychological relationships with his own past, present, and future. The nature of the evidence presented to support her interpretations differed in kind from the other presentations. Specifically, Silverman assigned semantic meaning to technique (for example, downward brushstrokes) thereby making it available for a hermeneutics of suspicion when convenient, while similar instances of techniques, such as downward brushstrokes in other paintings, were left unmentioned. In sum, Silverman's attempt to provide a totalizing framework for Richter's life and work by combining the political and the therapeutic in a manner that is totalizing and reveals the deep meaning available only to the interpretive gaze is modernist to the hilt. Not coincidentally, her interpretations are cast in an ironic mood; naturally this claim does not mean they are wrong (although I think they are). But given how adamant they are, it is simply the case that there has been silence about them from those surrounding Richter, at least in print.

During the question period that followed Silverman's presentation (and that is included in the video on the Richter website), one could sense that not everyone was convinced, but basically no direct engagement with her views took place, at least in public.[5] The event was taking place in Britain after all, and everyone was on good behavior. When I e-mailed some major participants, they agreed with my hesitations, but they have not made their views known publicly.

Pathos

I have taken up parts of Richter's work and the critical apparatus that has been elaborated around it as an instance that provides the opportunity to test the parameters of a contemporary mood and mode.

Consider the following statement by Hubertus Butin: "Richter has created a distance between painter and viewer. In so doing, the depicted event becomes a subject of reflection."[6] One way to understand this quotation is that it is a renewed assertion for the relevance of the traditional function of art: moral uplift or civic lessons, exemplary figuration of persons or scenes, or most broadly the function of art as a pedagogical *Bildung*.

Butin himself makes a compelling case earlier in the lecture just quoted in which the claim appears that Richter's "candle" paintings cannot and must not be taken as direct imitations or repetitions of the *Vanitas* genre. Rather, Richter's over-painting of such figural images is designed to produce an interference with attempts to understand the paintings as merely continuous with this older iconographic lineage. Nonetheless, Richter can be seen to be deploying one variant of the function of *Nachleben* that puts into question not only the traditional understandings of these images but also modernist ones that would negate the former affect and significance entirely. It follows that to the degree this work of interference and re-assemblage "works" (for the artist or for a projected viewer), then the affect produced would be one of pathos. The form would both affirm and deny the tradition and its negation, leaving open the question of what remains to be worked with and over today.

Such *Pathosaffekt* functions on a number of levels. First, for the artist it provides a test of how to facilitate the ratio of the technical and the medium. The range of possible topics or themes susceptible to be treated as such in a crucible of testing would be vast. Consequently, the artist is obliged to make choices as to which theme he is drawn to explore and test himself with—how to decide on a specific topic in the large thematic field. In the genre of moral lessons in art, Richter chose the topic of *Vanitas*. As with the Romantics' connection to nature, which Richter felt free to take up once again because there was no danger, if the proper medium was explored, of simply returning to an earlier position of viewing or understanding. Strikingly, Richter clearly has chosen to draw attention to the theme of the futility and effervescence of worldly pursuits. The explicit stylistic inclusion of *Nachleben*, and the forging of a form that fits and renders visible the pathos of such an image, makes the image a contemporary one.

Constellations: Forms of Object Production

It is always a question of a constellation. An objective situation in itself, that is to say the simple, instantaneous seizing of a moment, does not contain in itself the element of its organization, the element that renders it concrete. That is why the discovery of objective situations presupposes the production of the means of their production, the forms of objective production.
—Alexander Kluge

Dieter Schwarz, one of Richter's longtime studio assistants and the curator of a Richter exhibition in Bern entitled "Variants, Cycles, and Series: Gerhard Richter's Use of Multiple Images," observes in the catalogue (doubtless with Richter's tacit concurrence) that "operating with variants, groups of works, and sequences of images is a salient feature of Richter's painting and can be observed almost throughout his entire oeuvre."[7] The use of series or variants is an old practice in Western painting; Richter can convincingly be seen to have devoted a great deal of labor to exploring different ways of establishing a fruitful relationship to older forms, techniques, venues, and practices without directly reproducing them. One might say that Richter stubbornly insists on taking up terms such as "landscape" or "the domestic"—which modern critics have disallowed as retrograde—and restively conducts experiments with multiple ways of producing contemporary variants. As Schwarz puts it: "Art has no more come to an end than has the world. Richter confronts himself and the viewer with uncertainty as to what the next move will bring and where the next step will lead."[8]

Richter engages in a judgmental phase of his prodigious products and experiments; he arrives at a conjuncture at which he considers some successful and others not. He has had precious little to say about this process: he just "knows."

Richter often takes up a term ("landscapes"), experiments with concepts (and techniques) so as to render visible a different referent (image), often requiring a distinctive medium (over-painted photographs, squeegee work on the layers of paint) in order to accomplish this fresh rendering visible. That referent at once bears some resemblance to the older portrayal or object in prior painting, while displacing how one sees things. What the artist produces, however, when he succeeds is just as visible, just as real—that is to say, "documentary" in Kluge's sense of the term—as were the prior modes or seemingly representational referents. Thus, by combining signs of the old, technological supports and new media of the new, Richter can be understood to be experimenting with rendering things visible in a contemporary manner—he creates objects with their own distinctive actuality.

This mode of relation and distance in Richter's work is perhaps most explicit and visible (but not restricted to this genre) in his taking up of motifs from German Romantic painting. On several occasions, Richter has made his views known on this topic in response to anxious critics. Friends (and others) have challenged him as to how he could possibly be doing what he was resolutely continuing to do—painting scenes of turbulent seas, cloud-shrouded peaks, forest scenes, and pastoral meadows.[9]

For Richter, the foundational dimension of his experimentations was to recalcitrantly refuse the strictures of modernism; the hard part was exploring how to develop forms in which these traditional topics (and, to an extent, styles) could be combined with the techniques, accomplishments, and blind spots of the ensuing two centuries. In a word, the problem for which in principle there were multiple solutions available was this: how to become a contemporary painter?

A further reason Schwarz cites for Richter's lifelong attraction to series, cycles, and ensembles is a decision the artist made in 1962: "To work with photographs is a search for a point of reference outside his own work, enabling him to free himself from the gestural self-referentiality of contemporary *Art informel* and to embrace an opposing notion of the image as mediated in more than one way."[10] This second form of mediation lends itself to contemporary stylization in its attempts to establish a ratio between past forms (Romantic, modern) and the necessity to stylize things differently if the fictive documentary telos of art (to invoke Kluge once again) is to remain vital. "The components of such groups of works as *Bach*, *Wald*, and *Cage*, hanging next to each other on the wall, can be understood as variants of an idea that could not be brought to a single conclusion."[11]

Such a form of objective production is the product of a restive experimentation, proceeding without knowing where it would end up. It was recalcitrant to the strictures that reigned normatively but not seeking to directly contest them. It sought a mode of secession not rebellion.

Richter (like many of his contemporaries in painting, writing, and theory) sought to de-subjectivize his work. Whether in Michel Foucault's "what is an author?" or in Roland Barthes's "The Death of an Author" a common problem was how to give form to the drive to move away from subjectivity, phenomenology, taste without discounting experience. The goal was to free oneself from what was taken to be the miasmas of bourgeois affect, sentiment, and consciousness. Richter accepts that challenge but adds to it what he considers to be a rejection of the miasmas of feeling and consciousness of the modernist avant-gardes.

Another motive for Richter's exploration and priming of technique comes into play here: Richter became known (and soon thereafter famous) for the way he used photography as an anchoring for his image work.[12] As many critics have observed, Richter's use of photography of ordinary scenes and objects disrupted the strictures of modernism on the impossibility of direct representation. Although it would be tempting to emphasize pre-digital photography with its "contact sheets," in fact this analogy would be misleading, because as Schwarz puts it, "Richter's photography is never linear sequences." His use of ordinary snapshots and their alteration yielded a form of second-order observation that opened up a range of means to render visible things of the world in their historicity but neither as direct representations nor as a means of multiplying perspectives.

Abstrakte Bilder

It is crucial to underscore once again that there is no direct linearity to Richter's work. It simply is not true that he moved from photography to abstraction for example, or from small to large paintings, or large to small, or historical to nonhistorical and the like. His restiveness—and his importance—cannot be accounted for in those terms. In fact, Richter had explored abstraction in a general sense of the term from his earliest days as an artist; his recently recovered *Elbe* paintings demonstrate his interest both in abstraction and in variations.[13]

> The term "abstract painting" here no longer denotes a chapter in the history of art; neither does it describe a development from representational images to nonrepresentational, autonomous images; still less does it refer to a kind of painting that uses freely invented forms to give visible shape to psychological phenomena. [. . .] Richter's abstraction has no organic dimension: it does not mark the culmination of a chronological development.[14]

Still, the narrative is now established, with a certain authority, that around 1980 Richter turned intensively to the problem of what a genre of "abstract images" might look like that differed from—but was fully conversant with the trajectory of abstract modernism—the American experience and experiments. Above all there are many dimensions of this work, one that is directly relevant here is a shift in practice or *technē*. Dieter Schwarz clearly identifies this topic. Richter "has adopted the practice of working out his initial ideas simultaneously on a number of canvasses of the same size."[15]

By so doing the artist developed a means of altering his work rhythm, of creating a different bodily hexis, and of striving for a different visual field—as subject matter, object to be attained—during the process of painting itself.

Entering a studio in which assistants have prepared three or four blank canvases is quite a different experience from entering and facing a single canvas or even a number of canvases on different walls. The latter example is standard practice if the painter is working on different paintings at the same time. For Richter, this mode is not one in which the paintings form a progressive series or cycle; neither does it constitute a mode of addressing variations on a theme. Rather, it is a distinctive type of ensemble. "The paintings thus went through the stages of laying-in, execution, and reworking (by scratching away layers of paint and spreading some areas with the squeegee) while they stood next to each other."[16]

This practice allows for different kinds of multiplicity in Gilles Deleuze's sense of the term; it establishes a frame and a practice in which heterogeneity and adjacency can be put in motion. "This process encouraged comparison, exposed weaknesses more clearly and, above all, anchored the images in a relational system, something Richter had missed after turning to abstraction."[17] This insistence on putting to the test, seeking relations, and suspending judgment for a time has been characteristic of Richter's practice for many years.

Motion

Unwilling to ground his abstract art either in the theories developed by early modernism or in gestural automatism, he was faced with two possibilities: to treat abstraction as a representation—to this end he at first used enlarged watercolor sketches—or to take the actual working process as a point of reference, employing observation of developments in neighboring paints to grant the work a stable foundation. These pictures did not form progressive sequences, and they did not work through variations on a theme or modulations of specific principles to create an overall context for each canvas, contrary to single pictures. Whenever canvasses threaten to become too systematic or subjective, Richter relies on the reality of the paintings themselves as the sole, most compelling criterion for advancing his work.
—Dieter Schwarz

There were many phases to Richter's restive experimentations in multiple means of producing objects and objectives.[18] One thinks, for example, of Richter's revisiting of his own work such as the books he has composed years apart on his trip to Greenland as a young man.[19] His repeated turn to color charts over the course of many years and his attention to changing capacities of photography and its associated technologies of reproduction and modification of what and how things can be rendered visible as objects are just a couple of other such returns and departures.

One metric they all seem to share, which seems to guide Richter in multiple different forms over the years, has been captured by Dieter Schwarz as follows: "The compositions resist both the contemplative and the analytic gaze, refusing to let the eye come to rest and revealing nothing of their origins."[20]

To the best of my knowledge, Richter and his commentators have not engaged with the critic Michael Fried, whose distinction between *theatricality* and *absorption* has played a central role in art criticism including photography. As the above quote indicates, Richter fled both poles from the start.[21]

Richter's Friends: (a) Blinky Palermo

We were never competitive, because we were so different. I could always respect that, that he could make something so quiet. That was all so alien to me.
—Gerhard Richter

During the 1960s the art world still valued the figure of the artist as a gifted and heroic individual, a faded ancestor of the Romantic artist, the bohemian and/or the activist artist.[22] It was becoming harder to avoid the fact that creations—of subjectivity as well as of artwork—required specific work venues, financial and institutional support at various stages of production, and coordinated means of dissemination. This process of the figure of the avant-garde artist becoming historical has been a multifaceted one. Here I present one series of episodes contributing, albeit tacitly, to the fraying of that figure as well as timid openings to alternatives.

In order to carry out such an analysis, though one with a diagrammatic condensation, it is useful to look at instances of collaborations among and between artists confronting this conjuncture. This examination is opportune when the artists are themselves self-conscious about the changing status of the figure of the artist: conjunctures when artists confront their relation to the present as an existential problem, a challenge, a task to be taken up and reflected on.

Instance, Episodes

An instance of such reflection on practice and identity can be found in the relationship between Gerhard Richter and Blinky Palermo. The humorous pseudonym refers to the name of the manager of the heavyweight fighter Sonny Liston.[23] The collaboration between these two artists is instructive insofar as it took place during a time (the mid-1960s and early 1970s) when a new form of heroization of the artist set in the rise of consumer capitalism and its consequent commercialization of the artist was gaining prominence in West Germany. It is also the historical conjuncture during which a complicated reaction to figures such as Joseph Beuys and the search for alternatives were under way.[24]

That decade was marked by an emergent marketplace for abstract art, especially in the new art galleries in prospering cities such as Düsseldorf and Cologne. This sectorial market growth was cast negatively as one aspect of the Americanization of Germany in multiple domains: among them, lifestyle, consumption, and the arts. Pierre Bourdieu's term *la distinction* applies nicely to this period of redefinition of taste in relation to class relations and geopolitics.[25] The differences from Bourdieu's approach, however, are important. They include attention to transitions in regimes of distinction. In addition to the general responses to shifts in the macro-conditions of the economy, society, and culture, there were micro-milieus in which partial solutions to broader problematizations were being located, specified, and experimented with in a type of testing and articulation.

The problem for young German artists during this decade stemmed from abroad: How to understand and relate to the culture industries writ large arriving from the United States? How to relate to the hegemony of the New York art scene? More specifically, for young painters the challenge was to decide on and forge some relation to a nascent art market and its institutions in Germany. Finally, there was the problem of how to relate to abstract art in its American instantiation. That last challenge, at its limits, turned on whether it was possible to be a modern painter at all. That is to say, had painting, once again, come to an end?

Conjuncture: Affinities

The last chapter of art historian Christine Mehring's exacting book *Blinky Palermo: Abstraction of an Era* is entitled "Collaboration with Gerhard Richter." No doubt the fame of Gerhard Richter (and the current reputational decline of Palermo) occasioned the inclusion of a detailed chronology of this intense friendship. Nonetheless, the periods of collaboration between these then-young German artists can be sketched out so as to make explicit elements of a series: creation/collaboration/mode/mood. The detailed history and much more on the specificities of the German context can be found in Mehring's monograph.

Just as Richter has assembled art critics and theorists with whom he maintains a studied closeness and distance, so, too, his multiple punctual collaborations with other artists (not uniquely painters) are revealing of problems and blockages, as he seems to have used them as exploratory equipment in times of stasis. How have collaborations contributed to Richter's gradual articulation of a restive and recalcitrant ethos of production of art and subjectivity?

Palermo and Richter were both born in East Germany, the GDR, although Palermo's family moved to West Germany when he was young. Richter, eleven years Palermo's senior, was raised and trained under the Soviet Socialist–dominated regime.[26] The content and impact of Richter's training in painting in Dresden as well as his formative relationship—distancing—to the ideology of East German socialism have by now been well documented.[27] He left the GDR in 1961.

By 2015, Gerhard Richter was the most successful German artist and must figure in any discussion of contemporary art in the world. Consequently, an ever-growing volume of scholarly work concerning his life, influences, and art flourishes; Richter has facilitated and encouraged this industry, increasingly inseparable from the art market as well as a medium through which this distinctive figure of the contemporary artist has been forged.

Not coincidentally, little has been published on Richter's personal life: his multiple marriages, his wealth, and so forth. Richter has carefully and skillfully managed gossip, publicity, seemingly understated self-promotion, and interpretation of his works for decades. Strikingly, he has not cultivated his persona as mysterious and hidden. Rather, he has succeeded in cultivating his personality and life—and having others promote the idea—as being of little or no interest. The only topic worthy of scrutiny in the discourse surrounding Gerhard Richter is his art. He is boringly (upper) middle class. One might well say that Richter has forged one variant of a possible figuration of the contemporary artist. In contrast, artists such as Palermo (or Sigmar Polke or Joseph Beuys), whose current reputations are limited, and who are no longer living, have had their personal lives scrutinized and foregrounded.

Episodes

After their encounter at an art fair in 1966 in Aachen, Richter and Palermo became friends. The friendship grew, enabling distinct intermittent periods of artistic collaboration over the subsequent five years. During this span of time, they came to know and trust each other. One could say that the familiarity and trust facilitated a confidence to experiment in a minimally guarded manner.[28]

This familiarity and trust extended to Richter's closely guarded family sphere. During the mid-1960s, Palermo was experimenting with the use of cloth as a medium in place of paint as well as a critical response to what was understood by these young Germans as an impasse of abstraction. Given Richter's subsequent fame, it is amusing and touching to imagine the two young artists examining fabrics together in department stores but probably not blending in with the other customers. Richter's wife at the time, Ema, sewed the fabric Palermo had picked out while the young artists drank coffee and discussed the things of the day and paintings.

During this time of readymades and abstraction, Richter produced a portrait (1966) of Ema—*Ema: Akt auf einer Treppe (Ema: Nude on a Staircase)*—a reference and homage to Duchamp's shattering of conventions of portraiture and cubism with his painting *Nude Descending a Staircase* (1912).

JS: Were you influenced by Duchamp when you painted the pictures *Woman Walking Downstairs* (1965) and *Ema* (1966) . . . ?

GR: I knew Duchamp's work, and there certainly was an influence. It may partly have been an unconscious antagonism—because his painting *Nude Descending a Staircase* rather irritated me. I thought very highly of it, but I could never accept that it had put paid, once and for all, to a certain kind of painting. So I did the opposite and painted a "conventional nude."[29]

Mood

How did the artists relate to each other and to the art world of the time? Later on, Richter is quoted in an interview as saying: "Palermo never spoke about his art in theoretical terms. [He] talked about art a great deal."[30]

This skirting of direct position-taking of a theoretical kind, given the raging theoretical debates about the modern art emanating from New York (and taken up by many young artists and gallery owners in Germany at the time), was equally a refusal to enter into the domains of absolutes, unbridgeable rivalries, rhetorically self-important stances of subjectivity, and the like. Both of these young men were in the "show, don't tell" mode by temperament and background.

Richter's stance toward theoretical discussions was always carefully crafted: while continuously eschewing position-taking with a certain distancing humor bordering on disdain, Richter nonetheless kept himself informed about current debates. He did so primarily, it seems, by cultivating and maintaining relations with sophisticated, amiable, and cutting-edge theorists such as Benjamin Buchloh. The same manner and affect would be given a modified form later in his career in his encounters with curators of the art world's major museums and galleries.

Richter called Buchloh "my teacher," while never directly engaging in the level of discourse of which Buchloh was a master. In their many interviews and discussions, Richter almost never agrees with Buchloh's theoretical statements, but he always does seem to pay heed to them. Richter was in fact simply telling the truth: Buchloh was his teacher, but what he learned from him was second-order observations about theory and the market and how to remain adjacent to both.

The comment on Palermo's making something "quiet" [German: *ruhig*] is intriguing. Certainly Richter was never "noisy"; perhaps the contrasting term is "restive." A further level of meaning is present: Palermo led a troubled and turbulent life ending at a young age with drugs and death. Whatever Richter was picking out as significant was not Palermo's daily existence but rather his relation to his artistic work and to the art world at the time.

This ethos stands in stark contrast to Beuys. Palermo's exit from Beuys's tutelage toward Richter certainly marks a move away from the heroic and avant-garde toward something quiet and quotidian as the site of creation and self-formation.

1966: Readymades and Abstraction

During the first period of friendship and collaboration in 1966, the two artists shared explorations of the status and near future of the intersection of abstraction, painting, and the readymade. Palermo was working with commercially available cloth while Richter was undertaking a series of experiments (which he would return to sporadically over the years) of the stan-dardized, commercially available, paint-color charts available in a store. Thus, the fabrics and the color charts can be seen as a quiet form of ready-made as opposed to Duchamp's "noisy" readymades, most famously a uri-nal. The different manners that each artist took up their materials trans-formed them not into overt challenges to the status of the art object—that had been performed for decades—but into abstract presentations (e.g., War-hol, *Campbell's Soup Cans*, 1962). Richter's color charts, for example, allowed him to have a random series of colors available that he could arrange and rearrange in multiple variations.

In his self-deprecatory style, Richter says of Palermo's fabric-covered can-vases: "There was an aesthetic quality which I loved and I could not produce but I was happy that such a thing existed in the world. In comparison my own things seemed somewhat destructive, without this beautiful clarity."[31] Richter's turn of phrase, his work seeming "somewhat destructive," is telling. Both artists were consciously attempting to be "somewhat destructive" of the reigning orthodoxy of readymades, of the current status of abstraction, and of the normative sense of the actual and near future trajectory of paint-ing. Both, to hammer home our theme, can be seen to have been searching to establish a reflective relation to their present. Presumably, a reflective re-lation could be "somewhat destructive" if it was moving past modernism's proudly destructive relation to painting's tradition.

The friends exchanged paintings: Palermo gave Richter "Greensleeves II— probably after a Coltrane version."[32] The reference might well have been a gesture to Ema, who, after all, had done the sewing while the two men knit their friendship.

Recalcitrant: With, Beside, Against (*mit, neben, gegen*)

The peers of Palermo and Richter focused on all the things that painting after New York abstraction could no longer be as the pathway to confront the problematization of macro-vectorial change. During the 1960s Richter had engaged in collaborations with other artists. His joint work with Sigmar Polke sought and received a great deal of attention. Mehring argues however that these collaborative undertakings had a different basis and yielded a dif-ferent affect than the "quiet" and "purity" of the exchanges with Palermo. She observes:

Woven through Richter's collaborations with [Konrad] Lueg and Polke is the ironic staging and dismantling of bourgeois conceptions of the artist as unique, heroic creator, endowed with special powers. Yet these stagings also act as protective buffers and betray their creators' anxiety about what ought to replace such outmoded concepts. Collaboration with Richter [...] was always about managing insecurities.[33]

Collaboration was a form to counterbalance the competition between these other artists. Perhaps the mode of the Palermo/Richter collaborations was "comedic" in the sense of temporary resolutions seen in a second-order frame.

1970: Transparency?

In 1970 Palermo and Richter submitted a project for the Olympic games of 1972 to be held in Munich: it was rejected. The Games were highly symbolic as they were the first to be held in Germany since the infamous 1936 games, which Hitler attended until Jesse Owens triumphed over his Aryan competitors and Hitler exited so as to not award this African American a medal.

Palermo and Richter proposed two projects: the Sporthalle and the Schwimmhalle. The buildings that won the competition are still standing today. They are connected to the main stadium with the passageway covered by a vast, transparent plexiglass roof. This complex of buildings was nestled into a large hillside. Television producers had lobbied for this arrangement as a background setting for interviews and panoramic shots.

Palermo and Richter proposed to dye the 1,350 windows of the façade of the Sporthalle twenty-seven different colors, distributed randomly, while they proposed that the Schwimmhalle have ten stripes in different dimensions and colors, probably meant to run around its circumference—the proposal explained that the "endless bands are functional and beautiful."[34]

The dyed glass central to Palermo and Richter's proposal would have been semi-transparent (or semi-opaque depending on one's viewpoint). This condition would have rendered it unacceptable to the television producers.

There was a further problem in their design.

The grounds and the buildings centered, in the architect's words, around an "open expanse, translucence and an open view," thereby projecting an image of transparency, optimism, spectacle and community—the opposite of the secrecy and darkness of Germany's past. Visitors who climbed the sixty-meter-high grassy hill on the edge of the Oberwiesenfeld would find beautiful views of the complex; but as locals could tell them, the peaceful hill had been created from the rubble left by the Allied bombing of Munich and was known as the *Schuttberg*."[35]

History counts: *Nachleben* lurk, causing trouble for the moderns.

This early moment of form-giving was probably not yet a *Pathosformel*. But Palermo and Richter accepted that the condition of modern painting was near the point of creative self-destruction. Eschewing the avant-garde confrontational heroism of some of their contemporaries, Richter and Palermo oriented their work to an anti-attitude to decoration yet consequently established a relation to the present that was proximate to the decorative. The decorative has consistently been a term of denigration to avant-garde artists as it was seen as acquiescing too much to pleasure and the commercial. Establishing a relationship to the decorative was a challenge: as Richter observed later, if his works at the time were not kitsch they were close to it. By the mid-1980s, Richter was clearer about what his challenges were and what they were not: he stated boldly that Warhol was not an artist. How therefore to move from the proximate to the adjacent?

In November 1970 Palermo and Richter left for a trip to New York. They stayed ten days instead of fourteen, as they were exhausted from walking but also from the experience of the city as the fount of postwar abstract art. Christine Mehring quotes them as saying that in New York they felt European as opposed to the "straight" Americans. Presumably "straight" means "shallow" or "simplistic."

Mehring observes:

Richter's detail self-reflexively enlarges and elevates the chief ingredient of painting to its sole subject, thus blinding the viewer to anything beyond itself. That self-reflexivity, along with the clarity created by Palermo's frame and the state of absorption engendered by Richter's details, is a traditional aspect of beauty in aesthetic theory.[36]

This claim seems inadequate. Richter has never proceeded in the direction of achieving "absorption" any more than "theatricality." The myriad twists and turns of Richter's restive experiments were always recalcitrant to one degree or another to an absorptive viewing. The distance a viewer might adopt in relation to his paintings was a constant theme of unease and a topic of experimentation. Even his famous, seemingly photo-realist paintings, such as the one of his daughter or *The Reader*, have perplexed and irritated art critics for their seeming accessibility to a middle-class audience. That accessibility was certainly desired by Richter, but it was also subtly interrupted as compared to a number of other genres in which representation and abstraction are at play and in a mutually synergistic relationship to each other.

Thus Mehring does seem to be going in the right direction when she underscores Richter's myriad experiments in the balancing act of verging on the beautiful throughout his long career. With regard to the *Ausschnitte* of 1970/71, she writes that they are "very small extracts (*Ausschnitte* ca. 1–2 cm from palettes or from paintings, which by way of their enlargements as paintings become non-objective appearances of indeterminate beauty.)"[37] The use of the term "indeterminate" is telling. Whatever Mehring may have meant by it, we can take it up in the Deweyian sense of addressing a logical breakdown. I cannot fully follow Dewey, however, in his aesthetic claims that the works of art are the consummate products of an age. Or can I? Can they be defining instantiations of an ethos?

Association, Affinity

Two of Richter's paintings hung next to a window in Palermo's studio— Palermo framed the window with lines.[38] Richter's small paintings were of a roll of toilet paper—a kind of readymade mediated through photography and hence marking a distance from Duchamp. Their placement frames the studio's window, thereby fulfilling or at least addressing the three functions of painting toward which the artists felt they needed to establish a mode of relating: reproduction, banality, decoration.[39] As one solution, the explicit second-order referencing to the discordant configurations of the actual (how to accept and refuse these elements) brought them into an assemblage.

In another better-known collaboration, one that was public, the two friends again brought together the painting of gallery walls and a double sculpture in a common work. Palermo painted two walls of a gallery space, building on a series of paintings of walls to highlight and disrupt the decorative that Palermo had been engaged with for some time. Richter provided two heads—one of himself and one of Palermo—on facing pedestals.[40] This installation, if one is allowed by the experts to call it thus, was a reference and a remediation of the ironic and biting display that Richter and Konrad Lueg had done shortly before, *Leben mit Pop. Eine Demonstration für den kapitalistischen Realismus* (1963). They organized a modern living room in a space in a department store with the kind of design they were seeking to undermine, and then the two artists sat on the sofas in the display presenting themselves as both first- and second-order observers. The tone was High German wit. The installation of Richter and Palermo was more in the comedic mode. It referenced the growing status of artists as heroes and media stars but in a gentler way. It was pleasing aesthetically. It placed the two friends as clearly separate but looking at each other in a remediated setting of a gallery space. There was, or the setting could be seen to have, a muted agonism. Each artist's work and skills were distinct, but bringing them together in this muted agonistic manner afforded something comedic in the sense of a temporary resolution.

Palermo and Richter's final collaboration is entitled *Telefon*. An expansive, intense yellow ground, silk-screened pristinely by Palermo, frames two small, stacked images printed in four-color letterpress by Richter—a blurred image of a telephone placed in a corner with its receiver on the hook and a reproduction, it seems, of one of the diptych lightbulb panels.[41] Mehring offers the following characterization:

> *Telefon* compresses everything these two artists had worked on and cared about in their short time together: the decorative, the monochrome, and the color yellow, all represented by the framing field; the sliding scale of abstraction and figuration; the commodity embodied in reproducible art, commonplace letterpress print, banal household object, and evenly printed sample paint; the conjunction of the traditional and the up to date, exemplified retrospectively by the two printing techniques set into a flat pictorial plane; collaborative strategies of both framing and juxtaposition; and, above all, communication without words.[42]

One can gratefully accept this synthesis except for Mehring's claim that "above all" this collaborative work was about "communication without words." This claim is misleading. Rather, the two artists had rendered one solution to a more general problem visible and by so doing opened up the possibility that it could also be "enunciable."

Richter observed that he and Palermo could

> . . . really just talk about *painting*. The main thing was about the surface of color or the proportion of color. It was impossible for me to talk with Polke about the opacity of color. With Palermo, yes.[43]

> And then we had this *sense*, what is good or bad—and that was something terrific! Something that was immediately understood, when one sees something—a picture—and one says: There is something to this! That is good. That was particularly good with him. Those were the times when art was not really relevant enough. Above all art was not socially relevant. Yes, that was bad, and we sometimes felt like reactionaries.[44]

Neither term has anything to do with communication; it was about disrupting communication or adopting a recalcitrant stance toward the very acts of rhetoric and communication. This effort became a constant, restive dimension of Richter's practice throughout his long career. He would draw critics close to say things of a theoretical nature and then refuse that effort to place him in a communicative frame. If there was a public involved in these actions, it could only be a future one.

After Collaboration

The afterlife of the artists' collaboration is best characterized as being in a comedic mode of temporary resolution, one in which it was known that the resolution was temporary and given form in a medium in which such reconciliation was best rendered in a second-order manner. The question of the *Nachleben* of this comedic collaboration lingers.

By the end of 1971, Richter was becoming successful and known, providing him with the resources to move into a bigger studio and to attend to his own work. Palermo also moved to another studio, one farther from Richter's, making their casual get-togethers more difficult and less spontaneous. He entered into a period of severe creative blockage. In 1973, he moved to New York before returning to Germany two years later. He died in early 1977, perhaps of a drug overdose.

Richter's Friends: (b) Sigmar Polke

Modern art and modern lifestyle were thus conjoined in a new partnership based on cultural reform and economic prosperity.
—Mark Godfrey

As we have seen, the mid-1960s and early 1970s in Germany were a time of questioning the place and shape of modern art and the figure of the artist as well as a time of informal experiments with collaboration.[45] For Gerhard Richter and many of his German contemporaries, a primary challenge at the time was how to relate to international art (its market, critics, established interpretations, leading representatives, etc.) as it entered into the nascent modern art scene in West Germany. There were a number of different dimensions to this situation. Given the reigning conditions of the waning of abstract expressionism elsewhere, the core challenge was the question: what should painting be as an art form? A central aspect of that challenge was the further question: how could the relations of figuration and abstraction be remediated?

In Germany, there was the additional challenge of the spread of motifs, styles, and references of twentieth-century painting and sculpture into the burgeoning realms of design and decoration that were a constituent element in the rise of consumer culture in German in the 1950s and 1960s. Sigmar Polke (1941–2010) and other young artists identified the incorporation of older modernist motifs into home furnishings as a violation of art as well as an obstacle to future creation.[46]

Abstraction had become a favored motif in home furnishings. As Mark Godfrey observes, abstract forms such as "kidney-shaped tables inspired by Kandinsky or Klee"[47] were associated in the young artists' eyes with "kitsch decoration and the desire for exotic escape."[48] As an art critic observed, "Abstract art now permeated the most common spaces of postwar life—office, boutique, home."[49] The challenge for young and ambitious artists was how to exit from this entanglement, this confusion of realms. Should one seek to destroy the possibility of assimilating art into the world of comfort and consumption? Should one find a means of secession? Either direction required not only creative thinking and practice but also a coterie of critics and venues to receive, accept, and promote such moves—if one were to flourish or at least survive as an artist.

Onward: Toward the Contemporary?

Richter's friendship and collaboration with Blinky Palermo was distinctive in its intimacy, its mutually explicit understanding of being noncompetitive, and its attempt to accept differences in temperament and types if projects. Richter's collaboration with Sigmar Polke played out differently. Their relationship and their collaboration was more directly conflictual; their friendship was taut, producing an agonistic space that was productive for a short time. We can characterize Richter's friendship with Palermo as one cast in a comedic mode of temporary resolution and amicable motion; the Polke collaboration would best be seen as cast in an ironic mode. The ironic mode situated the collaboration in a modal proximity to the modernism to which it was reacting by seeking to distance itself through modernist irony. Although the agonism of the painters never slid into sustained antagonism, its tone was cool both between them and toward their common object/obstacle.

These young artists shared an understanding as well as an affect that the New York school and its associated art critics had played themselves out. What had once been a powerful and innovative movement was becoming a historical reference as it was visibly and without much friction being incorporated into the emerging consumer and corporate cultures.

Additionally, these young Germans were concerned and harried by the fact that derivative styles drawn from the signature motifs of abstract painting had become incorporated as marks of distinction for the rising German middle classes. For artists who stylized themselves as modern, avant-garde, and at odds with middle-class vulgarity, art and the artist could retain their distinctive status only if their work and their persona could not be taken up as decoration.

Consequently, the challenge for these artists was how to escape the encompassing grids of distinction and commerce that were taking shape and gaining traction. How should an artist relate to the growing sense that abstract painting was passing into being a historical style? Was there a successor to it or was it the end of the road for modern painting?

Association & Association

During the 1960s the art scene in West Germany was in turmoil; others, specialists, have covered the many movements and events—with their crossings of art, politics, and personalities—in great detail.[50] These years were the crucible or *foyer d'expérience* for Richter's coping with the West—he left the GDR in 1961—and more specifically how to become an artist and a successful one.

These young artists were confronted with the challenge of what to paint. They were also confronted with the challenge of finding venues to exhibit their work. They were equally confronted with the challenge of managing the critical and public response that they sought both to stimulate and to modulate. Richter, Polke, and others joined with Konrad Lueg (later Konrad Fischer, who became a gallery owner and sponsor of the new art).

In May 1963, Richter, Lueg, Polke, and several others applied to use an empty space owned by the city of Düsseldorf and were granted space by city officials to have a collective exhibit. They assiduously defined and solicited an audience of those they considered influential or potentially so in making the new art visible to a public. In order to do so, they sent out individual invitations with handcrafted stamps, each bearing one of a list of current names: "Pop art? Imperialist Realism? Anti-Kunst? Neo DADA? Junk Culture? Common Object Painting?" Elger characterizes their efforts as follows: "By co-opting contemporary art speak and using it as filigree, the artists sought to demonstrate the currency of their own artistic position without having to define it conceptually."[51]

The event was a success, drawing a large audience.

Now that an opening had been achieved (and sustained by more elaborate publicity stunts in the following years, including the famous "Capitalist Realism" show), the challenge of what to paint came more to the fore among and between the artists as well as for the emerging critical apparatus and eventual market. Richter and Polke were both keenly attentive to all of these dimensions of the emerging and still vulnerable art scene in West Germany.

Modern Art, Degenerate Art

Sigmar Polke contributed a painting to a 1968 exhibition entitled "Modern Art." Mark Godfrey observes in his illuminating chapter in "From *Moderne*

Kunst to *Entartete Kunst*: Polke and Abstraction," the MoMA catalogue of the 2014 Polke exhibition, that the painting could well have fit the image of a once-removed observer ("spectator" is Godfrey's term) at the time of the state of modern art. Polke's canvas is abstract, vaguely in the Kandinsky mode, to which Polke added a splatter of bright purple paint. As this purple was not identified with the usual palette of abstract painting, it stands out as a commentary and a disruptive gesture.

Godfrey goes on to argue that a good deal more than a splash of a color uncharacteristic of high modernist painters was at stake. He politely contradicts the interpretation of Polke's painting and the exhibit offered by the preeminent interpreter of postwar German painting, Benjamin B. H. Buchloh. Buchloh used the painting as the cover for a catalogue of a retrospective exhibit of Polke's paintings that he had organized. Buchloh wrote, "We find gestures of Modernist painting emptied, made empty by parodistic repetition."[52] It is true that by quoting many modern artists' trademark stylistic signatures, Polke seemed to be signaling that they had become clichés and no longer carried any avant-garde or visual power. This move could be taken to be, as it is by Buchloh, one of rejection through parody.

It would instantiate a banalization of formerly avant-garde motifs and styles by picking out specific motifs and repeating them in different ways, thereby rendering them as predictable and standardized elements of a style that no longer carried critical energy.

Godfrey convincingly rejects Buchloh's interpretation. Granted, the repertoire of motifs of high modernism, especially of abstract paintings and practitioners, can be taken up as an established apparatus. By so doing, however, the artist could approach such an apparatus analytically, parsing it into its elements and relationships. These could be rendered visible and thereby made available for reexamination and recombination. Perhaps it might then become possible to shape a different relation to the present of genuine significance. Parody is a settled and distanced relation. Polke was looking for a form of remediation and reassemblage, a reinvigoration of a heritage that was still animate, if barely so.

At the time, neither Polke nor Palermo nor Richter claimed to know whether and how such reanimation might be successful, creative, and freeing. Their efforts, however, were not simply parodic. Godfrey argues that taking Polke simply as a parodist misses his true ethos; he had a real affection for many of the artists from whom he was taking signature motifs. He was seriously engaged with disengaging from the reigning conditions of visibility and the uses to which they had been put. Whether Polke and his cohort would find an exit through this analytic and ironic approach was in no way assured.

Problem-Space

The Nazis had identified abstractionist tendencies (among others) in painting as "degenerate" (*entartet*). However, the return and approval of abstraction in the arts in Germany should not be understood as simply a rejection of the Nazis. The situation was more complex and overdetermined. Abstract painting also provided a distancing from the GDR's rigid rules of aesthetics. If there was a need *not* to dwell on the past in Germany, especially in representational forms, then abstract art fit part of the bill, but only part of it.

For Polke and others, embracing Kandinsky was no substitute for coming to terms with the Nazis. The problem was to take the stock motifs of modern art and disrupt or at least make visible their betrayal in commercial products. Polke's deconstructive use of motifs was a reference not only to the Nazis and the Soviets but also to the ready acceptance of abstract art by sectors of the German middle and upper-middle classes. The flies in the painting, the critic explains, "might stand for artists feeding off the past, or for the German bourgeoisie feasting off their beloved *Moderne Kunst*."

Godfrey argues, however, that Polke's main aim was not simply parody or refusal. Rather, he sees Polke engaged in a process of simplification so that he can work more clearly with and enjoy modernisms basic components.[53] In his notebooks the artist was working on a repertoire of abstract elements and forms. "For Polke," Godfrey says, "the process was not about arriving at the essence of the form but a way to corrupt an image and create something new with it."[54] How to bring art back to a present that was not consumerist or theoretical? Another limit on the parody or dismissal of modern art in its abstraction was Polke's close friendship with Blinky Palermo, who was a great admirer of Kazimir Malevich and some Americans like Barnett Newman. According to Godfrey, "It seems impossible that Polke would have laughed off the artists that Palermo looked up to."[55]

Paths ahead or back seemed blocked.

Negative Value

In 1982 Polke presented at Documenta 7 a series of paintings entitled *Negative Value I–III*. In this series he turned to techniques of "image disruption" using chemicals, photographic materials, and various types of paints and surfaces.[56] Some of his paintings looked different depending on where the viewer stood; this approach was an explicit attempt to disrupt any "totalitarian" overview or positionality.

Polke experimented with diverse materials and processes; in a sense, his studio became a laboratory. The materials determined or at least interrupted the painting process. This procedure might well have been aimed at removing the painter's direct subjectivity. It also turned the viewing of paintings into an experience and an experiment; the goal was not transparency. Reinventing abstraction also meant degenerating it by rejecting Clement Greenberg's core modernist claim that abstraction was the result of each medium's necessary specification of its separate areas of competence, which for painting meant flatness, the shape of the canvas, and opticality. Polke's experiments with other media (film, photography, etc.) disrupted and refused this purity. He sought to bring photography and painting into one medium as he did with abstraction and figuration.

Richter experimented with photography and painting, but despite their interplays and interfaces they remained in his work different media. Polke opposed that approach and sought to meld them.[57]

What direction did Richter take (in addition to his collaborative exchanges with Palermo)? The one he chose to publicize was his so-called detail paintings of 1970–71. As Richter later characterized them to his biographer Dietmar Elger, they consisted of

> very small details, ca. 1–2 cm squared, of palettes or from paintings that through enlargement take on an abstract appearance or uncertain "beauty" as images. In contrast to the modern comic elegance of Lichtenstein's brush-stroke paintings, the "details" clearly do not reproduce anything but the illusion of a kind of painting we might think to find in the nineteenth century but that never actually existed, or never existed with such emptiness. Despite my reservations, what I like about these detail paintings is that they are so radically Not-Painting, as only a reproduction

can be, insofar as it did not recall an actual image (the reservations: they are so likable, decorative, and interesting that their actual achievement and their antistance will be overlooked).[58]

This foray into Not-Painting painting—of references to the past that were then negated if the viewer took them up, its audacity of reproducing nothing actual—was certainly conceptually rich, if not artistically engaging per se for long.

Richter's caution about the fact that these works might be seen as agreeable and potentially available for decorative motifs was rooted in the countermovements of the time. Yet, he took that risk. He writes: "I was certainly aware that this was a tricky business—if not kitsch, then something approaching it. So I fully expected someone to come along and pick at the scab. And that turned out to be Polke."[59]

The casual reference to someone coming along to attack him was obviously not casual but a calculated risk Richter was by this point willing to take.

Elger describes the break between these two young artists as follows:

In 1971, Polke loaned a work to Richter's retrospective at Kunstverein für die Rheinlande und Westfalen in Düsseldorf, and he stopped by as Richter was installing the show. Upon surveying the new landscapes and seascapes . . . he remarked dismissively (according to Richter), "Why don't you just go ahead and paint some more trivia like that?" Richter, who was already insecure about the paintings, realized then just how far apart he and Polke had grown. Polke no longer seemed interested in his work, and that, for Richter, was what finally ended their friendship.[60]

Whether he cast it in these terms or not, Richter was parting company with the West German avant-garde. While this turning was no doubt personally trying, it marked Richter's commitment to following his own muse. This claim is not at all to say that Richter chose to be a Romantic; in fact, his commercial success was solidifying. Richter was becoming a Name.

Object 2: *War Cut*

I absolutely avoided expressing an opinion, which is completely useless here and obstructs the attempt to come somewhat closer to the truth. In addition, my opinion is almost certainly just as wrong as that of my friends who almost all greatly simplify matters, condemning the war and grumbling about Bush in a way that is closer to Kitsch. That is not my way.

—Gerhard Richter

Richter's book-length assemblage *War Cut* was catalyzed by the American invasion of Iraq in 2003.[61] In the *War Cut* book, Richter uses a large abstract painting he had done a long time previously and subsequently photographed and reproduced in multiple small images. For *War Cut*, he collated these smaller images with sections of articles from the German press that appeared during the initial days of the American invasion.

War Cut, published in 2004, was Richter's response to the invasion of Iraq by the United States and its allies. The book consists of collages: 216 photographic details of Richter's 1987 painting *No. 648-2*, accompanied by an equal number of newspaper articles from the *Frankfurter Allgemeine Zeitung* on 20 and 21 March 2003, the first days of the war. *War Cut* was published first in German and subsequently in French and English, retaining the German-language version of the newspaper articles.[62] Consequently, the German book should be distinct from the French and English editions; or, rather, the French and English editions should be seen as further refinements of Richter's undertaking, with the explicit referential language blunted even more than in the German edition.

The following is drawn from an interview done in April at Richter's Cologne studio by Jan Thorn-Prikker, a freelance critic and the editor of *Kulturjournal*, a cultural magazine of the Goethe Institute in Munich.[63] The translation is by Tim Nevill. I have taken the liberty of rewriting Thorn-Prikker's questions as well as rearranging Richter's answers without changing any of his words.

Paul Rabinow: What moved you to do this work? How did you assemble it? I gather the painting was an older one done in the 1980s that you were ambivalent about, and not at all sure it was good. Despite your reservations it was purchased and displayed by the Musée d'Art Moderne de la Ville de Paris. Why did you return to it?

GR: About two years ago I took close-ups of the work in the museum without knowing what I might use them for. When the war started, I heard all these conflicting opinions. I thought newspaper reports were impotent and ineffectual as everything else in the face of catastrophe but their plain presentation of the facts consoled me.

PR: Would you agree that you had a visceral response to the events but felt that the dominant critical forms were unsatisfying as responses? For you, direct representational responses and denunciations were ineffectual and banal at best. Was your goal to discover a different form of critique? How did you proceed?

GR: My layout determined what I included or didn't include. It was not something I had specifically in mind before I started. I wanted to vary the layout, to move from empty to full and back again. I had a general plan, a sense of balance. But the specific arrangement evolved as I worked on it, until at some stage there were 324 pages. I read most of the texts only after I placed them with the pictures. I read them as literature, which was very pleasing. I was not looking for straightforward narrative, which is maybe also why I chose that particular abstract painting. Some of my other abstract pictures are less ambiguous. Their atmosphere is either very agitated or tranquil or almost story-like in their narrative flow, so that they seem nearly representational or surreal. This picture had none of that. It was close to being uncommunicative, which I don't mean negatively.

PR: Hence the newspaper writings about conflict were juxtaposed with paintings that were originally not about strife. Assembling them gradually seems to have brought the elements of the painting and the texts into a common frame.

GR: "War Cut" only very indirectly involves reality. Even the facts in the newspaper articles somehow become unrealistic in this context. I removed the headlines and bylines from the articles. I respect the writers. But I like to think that maybe by removing the headlines I contributed toward having these texts read as literature. It would be like taking a newspaper photo and putting it in a museum as an oil painting, which is I suppose what I did with Baader-Meinhof [RAF].

PR: Perhaps you were seeking to see what would happen if you brought realistic writing into a form with a disarticulated abstract painting? Could this process make something different happen? Could it open up a different range of realism and affect, fiction and nonfiction?

GR: My approach to form is very simple. Whatever is real is so unlimited and unshaped that we have to summarize it. The more dramatic events are, the more important the form. The way texts and images influence one another; change their meanings, with the images changing incomparably more because they are much more open and ambiguous.

PR: If I understand correctly, the work of assemblage does not follow a plan. It requires a set of materials, in your case preexisting ones, which you bring together until something appears to be happening that pleases you.

GR: Form is all we have to help us cope with fundamentally chaotic facts and assaults. Formulating something is a great start. I trust form; trust my feeling or capacity to find the right form for something. Even if that is only by being well organized. That too is form.

PR: How does this process of following and guiding a work in-formation relate to exterior events? It seems to be neither directly referential nor disconnected from events and the mood of the present as you and others experience it albeit in different ways. Was your form-building related to chance?

GR: As for chance consider John Cage. His musical compositions were never a total appropriation of a chance acoustic event. He devised an ingenious system to build structures from dumb abundance. And he devoted even more skill to giving form to this succession of sounds. That is the absolute opposite of chance, nature, and rubbish. In this case the facts are so overpowering, the contents so crucial, therefore the form is all the more significant. We need it simply to be able to deal with the subject matter. I wanted to try and see this war from a completely different angle. Admonitions, protests and such are not my thing.

PR: Many of your works are affectively complicated and hard to discern and name. They seem to produce a range of intense moods into what might be called a zone of viscosity. They seem to arise out of experiences characteristic of your generation that linger on and somehow must be taken up.

GR: Yes, these experiences are present like an underlying theme.

3

ASSEMBLING Abet and Facilitate

> Language can express only what language enables it to express.
> That is why all theory is absolutely circumscribed, almost un-
> usable, but always dangerous.
> **—Gerhard Richter**

Judgments concerning the quality of artworks are notoriously hard to establish and to evaluate. This situation is doubly difficult for contemporary
works of art. By this I mean that without the historical distance that art historians and market-driven critics require in evaluating paintings' aesthetic
importance or significance (itself of course historically mutable), it is a futile
undertaking to rank painters and paintings. The only domain in which such
an approach to stratification is plausible is one in which there are direct contests with fixed rules: each year we know who won the Super Bowl or the Pre-
mier League championship. Elsewhere, the leading standard for valuation
is the market. Remembering Kant's distinction between worth and value
leaves us questioning how to proceed.[1]

There is a further reason why aesthetic judgments of contemporary art
are also vexed. Ever since Theodor Adorno's challenges to the autonomy of
the aesthetic, the topic is one that art critics in the theory game must reckon
with.[2] The symbolic prestige of high theory makes critics anxious about
offering aesthetic judgments at all. The friendly interactions and discussions
over the years between Gerhard Richter and Benjamin Buchloh underscore
this point: Richter operates with aesthetic judgments every day in producing his own work as well as in his opinions about other painters, which are

often bold and unequivocal. Buchloh rarely if ever offers aesthetic judgments of individual works. except from time to time to express his personal preferences, but he does not hesitate to proliferate theoretical observations about art and history that Richter listens to but most often does not approve, sometimes disagreeing outright and sometimes skirting the topic. Of course, the validity of this claim in no way entails that Richter is right and Buchloh wrong (although frequently I agree with Richter).

Not being a licensed practitioner of either the art history or the art criticism professions, I will approach Richter's artistic work (and his opinions) in a different manner. I begin by wondering where a particular set of work that clearly has a referent to things happening or that have happened in the world falls within a series: episode / event / *kairos*. This query applies both to the happenings in the world and, in a different frame, to how the artist qua artist takes happenings as (tacitly) part of a series that includes and informs his (in this instance) judgments.

Assembling Objects

Understandably, a great deal of critical attention has been paid to Richter's series *October 18, 1977*. He had waited more than ten years to paint this series of scenes of the deaths in prison of members of the Red Army Faction.[3] Part of this critical attention arises from the return of figuration in Richter's work. In this collection of paintings, Richter took up press photographs of episodes in the fateful event and reworked them in his characteristic fashion of blurring and using subtle variations, especially of gray tones. Examining Gerhard Richter's attempt to render something visible—the suicide/murders of members of the Baader-Meinhof gang—provides us with an object and perhaps a lesson in how a restive *ēthos* can be put to work to bring new capacities in the world.

Robert Storr, for a time a curator at the Museum of Modern Art in New York (during which he organized a major Richter exhibition around the controversial *October 18, 1977* paintings), and subsequently dean of the School of Art at Yale, has written several monographs on Richter's work. Storr's prose is free of jargon (by art-world standards), and his interpretations are not contested directly by Richter, thereby providing at least the appearance of his endorsement of, or at least acquiescence to, Storr's interpretations.

A refugee from the former East Germany, Richter insistently presents himself as permanently and militantly nonideological and antitheoretical. Storr willingly takes him at his word and provides a lucid and reliable presentation of Richter's work. That American clarity, of course, guarantees neither the interpretation's veridical claims nor its comprehensiveness. It does, however, I argue, constitute a part of the dynamics of assemblage that Richter is restively designing, that is to say, shaping and inflecting.

Yet Richter rarely agrees with the aesthetic, veridictional, or ethical claims of Buchloh's jargonized, Adorno-like, high discourse. With a persistent regularity, in response to a theoretical assertion, Richter simply claims not to understand what Buchloh is talking about; at other times he directly disagrees. In these exchanges, Buchloh appears textually like a character out of Thomas Mann (more *The Magic Mountain* than *Doctor Faustus*, more Settembrini than Zeitblom) in his insistence on theorizing everything; he barely seems to notice, or in any case does not remark on, the fact that year after year, Richter refuses to acknowledge the core of his claims. This fact, of course, does not mean that Buchloh's interventions are erroneous.

It is admirable, if highly unusual, that this interpretive dissonance does not seem to stand in the way of their discussions, repartee, or friendship. Here is one example:

BB: It seems to me that you introduce process-related painting as just one of painting's many possibilities, while not insisting, as Ryman did, that it is its only aspect.

GR: Then why should I go to such lengths to make it so varied?

BB: Because you are setting out to call off all the aspects there are, like a catalogue; because you're really trying to pursue both a rhetoric of painting and the simultaneous analysis of that rhetoric.

GR: If all this were just a matter of display—the way the yellow, tatter-edged area rises up against the blue green background—how could it tell a story or set up moods?

BB: A mood? You mean it really sets up an emotional experience?

GR: Yes, and aesthetic pleasure, too.

BB: That's something different. Aesthetic pleasure I can see, but absolutely not a mood.

GR: So what is a mood?

BB: A mood has an explicitly emotional, spiritual, psychological quality.

GR: That's exactly what is there.

BB: Fortunately only in the weakest parts.

GR: Surely you don't think that a stupid demonstration of brushwork, or of the rhetoric of painting and its elements, could ever achieve anything, say anything, expresses any longing.

BB: Longing for what?

GR: For lost qualities, for a better world—for the opposite of misery and hopelessness.

BB: The longing to be able to present culture as a contemplative spectacle without losing credibility?

GR: I might also call it redemption. Or hope—the hope that I can after all effect something through painting.

BB: Again, this is all so generalized; effect in what sense? Epistemological, emotional, psychological, political?

GR: All at once, I don't know . . .

BB: It's the contradiction of knowing full well that the means you are using won't achieve what you aim for, and at the same time not being prepared to change those means.

GR: That's not a contradiction; it's a perfectly normal state of affairs. The normal mess, if you like. And that couldn't be changed by choosing different means and methods.

BB: Do your paintings invite acts of faith, or analyses? What matters more to you?

GR: Either would be fine with me. In your case they invite you to analyze; others find them an invitation to perform acts of faith.[4]

Seeing and Saying

It is as if Richter is acknowledging and affirming the unsurpassable existence of a critical discourse, whether or not he agrees, concurs, or is bypassed by it intellectually or otherwise. Richter, after all, is not operating primarily in the veridical field of true and false: he is a painter. As with his abstract paintings—*abstrakte Bilder*—he is making a space for, making visible, rendering framed, a thing of the world: color and line and volume in one medium and theorizing, concepts, casuistry, and sophism in the other. Both domains exist: they are things of the world, the modern world as well as some contemporary scenes. Richter is assembling some of the discursive vectors that surround his work; whatever his motives (friendship, patronage, marketing, curiosity, etc.) he is assembling diverse and heterogeneous elements. Through form-giving, he is creating something. That, after all, is what he does.

One response to this interpretive discord would be to attempt to mediate it. For example, one might try to bring the critics together at a symposium, let them speak, and then have a moderator propose some form of conciliation. Such hermeneutically guided discussion and communicational triage would lead in this case, as in so many others, to a thin soup. Regardless, neither required American-style politesse, nor persevering German clarification, nor arch French stylization would further, in my opinion, what Richter is abetting and facilitating.

Storr provides one powerful alternative interpretation when he analogizes Richter's approach to that of Brecht. Storr writes:

> Rather than identification with the characters, Brechtian drama creates distance between them and the audience; rather than involving the public with the action, as was true in classical dramaturgy, it confronts the public with difficult choices; rather than smooth transitions from scene to scene it presents discontinuous self-contained episodes; rather than emotional release, it leaves the viewer with unsolved problems and persistent intellectual and spiritual discomfort. Richter's paintings do much the same.[5]

Richter's interviews and publications do much the same with his own critical work. Richter keeps these critical discourses in close proximity to his paintings, but he does so in such a way that the heterogeneity among the interpretations as well as between the discourses and the paintings is given a form.

Consequently, Richter assembles elements that act so as to cause one to question things ("who is more convincing?"; "Why is he talking to these critics?"; "Is any of this talk significant?"; "How does that swatch of green paint relate to this discourse?"). Although assembling problems is already a feat, perhaps a mark of something more is that at times we get a strong sense that the stakes are more than this problem of interpretation or that dispute over quality, but rather a problematization.

Assembling *October 18, 1977*

Ezra Pound's Modernist call to arms was "make it new." For Richter, a product of Utopia's ruin, it would seem that the precondition for making anything new—at least any abstract picture—is to make something old or evocative of things already known, so that the known style and the old ideal can be annulled, undone, unmade.
—Robert Storr

In mid-winter 1989, fifteen paintings were exhibited at a small museum in Krefeld (outside Cologne).[6] The museum was the former house of Mies van der Rohe, hence a tribute of sorts to high modernism. Buchloh observes:

> That this group of paintings was first exhibited in a building by Mies van der Rohe seems an appropriate historical accident, for Mies is the architect who constructed the only German contribution to public monumental sculpture in the twentieth century, devoting it to the memory of the philosopher Rosa Luxemburg and the revolutionary Karl Liebknecht, both of whom had been murdered by the Berlin police. The coincidence establishes continuity between a bourgeois architect in the Weimar state of the 1920s and a bourgeois painter in West Germany of the 1980s. And indeed both artists differ from most of their contemporaries in their ability to tolerate, in public view, the challenges to the very political and economic system with which they identify as artists.[7]

Yet one must wonder, as Buchloh does not, what it means to be a bourgeois in the twenty-first century. Mies had a clearer vision of how modernist architecture would accommodate capitalism and the persona of the architect than does Richter, even though Richter lives in comfort and his paintings sell readily at high prices. Furthermore, Mies's problems (political, aesthetic, and ethical) are not the same as Richter's. In fact, it is the whole world of political ideology including modernism that Richter is attempting to leave behind without forgetting it.

The overt subject matter of the series of black-white-gray canvases would be known to all Germans of a certain age and education: the officially proclaimed suicide or suspected murder in prison of two of Germany's most illustrious political terrorists. Richter's gray, black, and white paintings include portraits; scenes of the confrontation and arrest; the physical setting of the prison cells; the hanged body of Gudrun Ensslin; eerie, almost tender portraits of the leading woman, Ulrike Meinhof; and a funeral procession. Storr's claim that "studied separately, but even more so together, the fifteen paintings are among the most somber and perplexing works of art in modern times" is an uncontroversial one.[8]

Venue

The Museum of Modern Art in New York acquired the series in June 1995. Exactly how this happened is a subject of debate as there was a sense that a promise of sorts had been made to the Museum für Moderne Kunst in Frankfurt. There is the countervailing story, however, that the museum's trustees, one of whose members had been killed by the Red Army Faction, refused to pay for the paintings. Regardless, by shifting the context the paintings were placed within an art-historical series rather than as illustrations of a political interpretation; by shifting the venue of their presentation, the form of their presentation was altered. It is in this light that Richter's claim that neither political intent nor historical truth was at issue makes some sense. The paintings both evoke and annul the historical and political elements that would almost inevitably be evoked by viewers who were aware of these elements and had been moved by them in one fashion or another. As an act of memory, the paintings would be caught in a small set of possible associations.

We can agree with Storr that here Richter was as always trying to make something new. Part of the artist's capacity was to see that the paintings' actuality would change if they were located elsewhere as well as that he had the standing, power, and resources in the art world to make this transfer happen and seem worthy of debate.

By including a change of venue in his assemblage, and knowing that Storr would provide a certain reading while allowing Buchloh and others to provide quite different readings, Richter could be confident that the paintings stood a chance of retaining a lasting actuality. As he wrote:

This means that they are documents and they are not illustrative materials. . . . The reviews [in the United States] were inspiringly different from the German ones. Here one was so affected by the subject matter that the paintings were almost exclusively viewed in political terms — or even as a kind of family affair. . . . People abroad did not let their expectations and bias obscure their view of the paintings.[9]

Although it is clear what Richter means, it is more accurate to say that "people abroad" had a different and probably more diverse set of expectations that would obscure their view of the paintings in different and diverse ways.

Mode

We should take seriously Richter's disclaimer: "These pictures possibly give rise to questions of political content or historical truth. Neither interests me in this instance."[10]

He knows perfectly well that the pictures would give rise to questions, debates, accusations, and defenses of what they presumably represented in terms of political content and/or historical truth. Among the many things Richter was attempting to achieve was to move the debate away from remaining in a deadening perpetual oscillation between the polarities of politics and theory. Richter was neither aligning himself with the existing sides of the debate and the politics (he recognizes some validity or coherence for each), nor was he dismissing the whole affair. Rather, he was attempting to set something else in motion: make something taken to be past visual in the present. Perhaps we can affirm that his objective was to abet and facilitate objects, seeable and enunciable.

Richter refers to the paintings as a "leave-taking" (from violent struggles and ideology). Storr adds that the same is true of epochal and revolutionary criticism. Storr observes that the previous forms and norms of revolutionary criticism today function so as to conserve the past, not to challenge the recent past or near future.

"As historical paintings they remain eloquently unresolved; as a contemporary requiem they stop short of transfiguration."[11] They heighten or reawaken tensions, but they do not resolve them. Those portrayed are neither heroes nor antiheroes, as they would have been in the modernist tradition. Rather, there is an activation of memory, not its erasure—but such activation is not designed to achieve either a stable integration of positions in the present or a clear identification with past figures. If anything, these "somber and perplexing" paintings yield a range of troubled reactions.

Mood

The past, however, does not disappear: quite the contrary. The leave-taking is not from painting either—quite the contrary—but how is it done? And here, I believe, a contemporary form of *meletē* enters in. Crucial to this leave-taking is a mood shift. The Stoic practices of *meletē* were a form of preparation and preparedness, with a subset of these practices directed at composing a relationship to the future. The *praemeditatio malorum* was a specific form of preparation "realized through the test of the non-reality of what we actualize in this exercise of thought."[12] Preparedness was the exercise of thought upon thought, in this case focalized in and on the imagination and the flow of representations and associated passions. It was a test of reality and of one's relationship to that reality. In this instance, that reality was death, evil, and the incapacity to act directly on events and situations.

Let us remember that Richter was adamant, even indignant, when his friend Buchloh sneered at the possibility that he was attempting to create a mood in the *October 18, 1977* paintings and equally much, albeit in multiply different ways, in all of his work. Predictably, Buchloh was following the line of criticism of mood (*Stimmung*) as essentially antirational and politically nefarious, which Adorno (and Pierre Bourdieu) had articulated as an attack on Heidegger.[13]

So what is mood? The French scholar Gérard Genette, in a long chapter on "mood" in *Narrative Discourse: An Essay in Method*, quotes the definition of "mood" from the authoritative French dictionary *Littré*:

> The term [i.e., "mood"] is used here with a sense very close to its linguistic meaning, if we refer, for example, to this definition in the Littre [*sic*] dictionary: "Name given to different forms of the verb that are used to affirm more or less the same thing in question and to express the different points of view from which the life or the action is looked at."[14]

This capacity to vary points of view is the function of narrative mood. Mood turns on designing and structuring the place and function of distance and perspective. But how specifically is mood put to work in narrative? The answer is that it can be deployed in many different ways. Of those diverse ways, the pertinent trope for the problems we have been considering is metalepsis. Metalepsis (*transumptio* in Latin) is an old trope that appeared in the ancient handbooks but has come to occupy a much broader and more inventive place in modern literature, albeit one that has received less critical attention, including from those who practice it.

Genette tells us that technically metalepsis is achieved through "the act that consists precisely of introducing into one situation, by means of a discourse, the knowledge of another situation."[15]

Its strength and its unsettling dynamics arise from its deployment of "a boundary that is precisely the narrating (or the performance) itself: a shifting but sacred frontier between two worlds, the world in which one tells, the world of which one tells."[16]

Staying on the verge in a metaleptic narrative is extremely difficult. "Whence the uneasiness that Borges so well puts his finger on: 'Such inversions suggest that if the characters in a story can be readers or spectators, then we, their readers or spectators, can be fictitious.'"[17]

Metalepsis is troubling, Genette argues, because of its simultaneously unacceptable and persistent insistence that the extra-textual is always textual. What is bothersome here is the challenge that "the narrator and his narratees—you and I—perhaps belong to [the same] narrative."[18]

Achieving an effective metaleptic narrative requires more than technical skill. It requires the ability to effectively produce a mood: one in which distance and perspective are troubled, uncertain, and significant; one in which the spectator feels herself observed and involved.[19]

A metaleptic trope has an additional and significant characteristic. Metalepsis is the only one of the canonical tropes that operates in an explicitly historical register. Metalepsis takes up the past, or an aspect of the past, or rather the enduring presence of something past, and makes it function within a different narratological milieu—above all an assemblage for Richter—thereby subordinating it to a different function and thus transforming it and making it present.

One germane aspect of this historical and transformative mode of dealing with unresolved tensions has been explored by the American literary and cultural critic Harold Bloom, especially in his well-known *The Anxiety of Influence*. Metalepsis, he writes, is a return of the dead, but very much in the poet's own dress, his own colors.[20] This sentence sounds as if it were written about some of Richter's work, not only his *October 18, 1977* paintings but also others, such as his infamous painting of his "Uncle Rudi" in his Nazi uniform.

Such making-present can be done in any number of ways. Its general form, however, is beautifully captured by James D. Faubion when he says metalepsis is "a calling up of the past precisely in order to acknowledge at once its weight and its failure, its incapacity to determine the present and the future, which is what allows it to establish a mood of hope, of positive possibility."[21] Finally, this mode of re-presenting is not ironic—the modernist mode par excellence. It seeks to do more than negate or displace or trouble the apparently real. The challenge of the metaleptic in literature and, it seems, in some painting and philosophy is not to freeze distance and perspective. Rather, it is to provide the elements through which a form of possibility is made actual through the bringing into the present of something (sign, event, mood, etc.) that has passed but remains pertinent and salient. The skill is making this feat happen without precisely fixing exactly how it remains pertinent and salient. Unless there is a metaleptic implication of the viewer into the presentation, the effect will remain either nostalgic or ironic.

Thus, in contradistinction to Buchloh's claim that history painting as a genre is no longer possible for a true artist, one can see Richter's series as an attempt—metaleptically—to paint historically without the comfort of a philosophy of history or an understanding of representation in art either as giving direct access to the world or being thoroughly incapable of doing so. Storr underscores this point when he says, "The problems it poses are out of a tradition, and they manifest the tradition's struggle to adapt to new circumstances."[22]

The challenge is how to make history painting contemporary or more accurately how to present historical elements in a contemporary assemblage such that new visibilities and enunciable things become actual, inducing motion and affect.

Reciprocal Lacunae

For in each testimonial production, in each act of memory, language and image are absolutely bound to one another, never ceasing to exchange their reciprocal lacunae.
—Georges Didi-Huberman

Gerhard Richter approached the problem-space of what we have been calling *Streitschrift* and *Streit-Bild* space (and its generic problem of the relations of "*le visible et l'énonçable*") on a number of different occasions over the course of many years.[23] Some of these interventions are quite famous in terms of his series of paintings—for example, the deaths in Stammheim prison of members of the Baader-Meinhof group as previously discussed. But there are other series that have received less attention. These include a series based on four photographic images that the French art historian Georges Didi-Huberman recovered; they were taken at the Birkenau extermination camp perhaps by one of the *Sonderkommandos*, the work units made up of Jewish inmates forced to carry out the worst, most horrific duties in the camp. It seems probable that one of them succeeded in taking four very blurry images of a bunch of corpses in an open field behind a copse of birch trees—hence the name "Birkenau."

In the fall of 2013, Didi-Huberman accepted an invitation from Richter to visit his studio. We do not know precisely in what terms Richter wrote to the French art critic. From Didi-Huberman's response—a letter to Richter written several months after the visit and included in the catalogue of an exhibition—it is clear that the motivation for the invitation was directly connected with Didi-Huberman's book *Images in Spite of All* (*Images malgré tout*). The book is a presentation of four photos. These images were somehow smuggled out from the camp—it is not known how or by whom—and they are the only preserved images of the corpses the camp had been designed to produce in industrial-scale quantities—and to assure that they were not seen by those outside.

The problem of images of the Nazi extermination camp at Auschwitz/Birkenau is stated by Didi-Huberman as follows: aside from distant aerial views, "*not one single view* exists of crematorium V—situated in a copse of birch trees, from which Birkenau gets its name—that is not obscured by some plant barrier."[24]

There are several layers of interpretation and signification embedded in this statement of fact. The first is the bald statement about existing images. The second underscores the obstruction created "by some plant barrier." It is the combination of these two that draws Didi-Huberman's attention. It also draws the attention of other critics as well, not to mention our own.

It is absolutely not the case that the horrific activities of this extermination camp were not photographed or documented. In fact, the Nazis operated two photographic laboratories at Auschwitz. As is well known, the regime's documentation in other media was obsessional. "The Nazi administration was so anchored in its habit of recording—with its pride, its bureaucratic narcissism—that it tended to register and photograph everything that was done in the camp, even though the gassing of the Jews remained a 'state secret.'"[25]

However, the prolific production of documentary images by the Nazis did not survive. The reason for this fact can be taken up in the frame that Didi-Huberman provides: "Analyses of the concentration camp have long converged on the fact that the camps were laboratories, experimental machines for a *general obliteration*."[26] The machinery of obliteration included machinery to obliterate that machinery. It was put into operation as the defeat of the Third Reich loomed over the guardians of its documentation.

Visit and Exchange

Richter had a copy of Didi-Huberman's book and a reproduction of one of the Birkenau photos pinned to the wall of his studio. Nicholas Serota, chief curator at the Tate in charge of the large retrospective of Richter's work, after seeing the photo pinned to the wall in the studio, asked, "Are you going to do something with this?" Richter replied: "Well I'm haunted by it and I want to do something with it but I don't know what to do with it, because it's non-representable on the one hand but also it needs to be, it's an absolute part of existence, certainly for Germans in any case."[27] The problem and the challenge could not be stated more succinctly.

Didi-Huberman describes his visit to the artist's studio. He remarks on its cleanliness and order. We see in Didi-Huberman's photographs, reproduced in the catalogue of the Richter exhibit in Bern, the whiteness of the studio walls, the carefully arranged and labeled paint cans, the ladder poised near a white wall ready for the artist's use. The photographs are all devoid of the artist's presence or any human activity. Didi-Huberman underscores the four blank canvases on two walls. In his letter to Richter after his visit, he writes:

When I entered your studio last December 19 [2013], there were, hanging on the walls, four large, empty pictures. Desperately blank. Waiting. But, for what? I immediately understood that the object of your invitation was precisely these "empty pictures"—and more fundamentally, the *waiting for images*, or pictures that do not exist, or not yet, or perhaps never will exist. In short, did you invite me over in order to show me that you had not yet painted these four pictures? This is an extremely unusual invitation and, therefore, extremely serious.[28]

In his rambling, meditative reflections on his visit to the studio and to the artist and the nature of the invitation that had been sent to him, the critic sorts through a range of explanations.

One that is compelling is his identification of the theme of the restive attention to an exit (*aus*). At the most literal level this hoped-for leaving can be seen as a type of waiting for an image to begin to take shape and that somehow draws the artist to the canvas or canvases. Richter says explicitly that he is still waiting for a way to introduce the Birkenau photos into a contemporary image. It has been sixty years.

> **GR:** In order to capture the [horror] of the photographs, one summer day in 1944, probably only a few minutes were needed. Yet sixty years were necessary to grasp the importance of what this "insight" might mean for us.
>
> **GDH:** On December 19 of last year, you had invited me to come to see that you had not yet painted these four paintings: four photographs of Auschwitz-Birkenau. Such was—and is—the common theme, still very silent, of our meeting. [. . .] But you have never made a painting based on the Holocaust.
>
> **GR:** Not directly, no. I made a few attempts, and Konrad Fischer and I planned an exhibition at one time. I can't come up with a suitable form, can't find a way of presenting it so that it's bearable and not just spectacular. [. . .]
>
> **GDH:** Did you consider, nevertheless, making a painting from that image?
>
> **GR:** Yes, often.
>
> **GDH:** Did you begin?
>
> **GR:** No, it has a huge impact as a small, framed photograph. I couldn't add anything to it.[29]

A Curtain of Trees

Mark Godfrey, one of the Tate Modern curators of the 2011–12 exhibition *Gerhard Richter: Panorama*, in his fine presentation, "A Curtain of Trees," provides compelling insights into the background and meaning of a series of Richter's experiments. As Godfrey argues in his Tate lecture, there is a lineage of modernist criticism of abstract art that is vigilant about refusing the introduction, discursive or otherwise, of external references per se and especially reference, analogy, or metaphor bridges to nature.[30] He quotes Rosalind Krauss's essay attacking those who saw a Jackson Pollock painting entitled *Lavender Mist* as being "about" rain; Krauss regards the title (perhaps given by a gallery owner) as an unfortunate bit of irony that could only mislead those in search of figuration as well as those operating in anything but an ironic mood.[31] The dogma of high modernism was that painting was about painting: the practice, the material, and the oblique references, at best, to an internal tradition of those who came before in the recent past.

Parameters

Godfrey's first topic: for Richter "affect is more important than imagery."[32] Richter should not be approached, Godfrey argues, at a literal level of iconography. He is not a painter whose work contains a hidden significance carried in the images themselves. As we have seen, Richter frequently paints in series and ensembles; thus it is risky to take a single image as final and autonomous. Richter's paintings are the product of layering and transformation from an original state, be it one that is directly representational of objects or scenes, or one once removed as in photography, or ones multiply removed from representation and transformed over and over again as in many of the abstract paintings.

Godfrey's second topic is formulated as a problem: "could one make a radical painting from a traditional image?" I modify this formulation by asking: given the awareness of a long history of images, some of which now qualify within the art-historical discipline as traditional, how can they be taken up in a contemporary manner? Phrased in my technical language: given the inescapability of *Nachleben*, what are the techniques and *technē* available to give them a contemporary form?

Godfrey's third topic is a claim: "no matter what the desire for continuity with the past, one is left with a consciousness of a break that makes cohesion impossible."[33] The context Godfrey provides is an essay by Theodor Adorno.[34] This claim might well be pursued in a narratively tragic mood in which both the maker and the observer are admonished (by themselves) to never forget the fundamental and irrevocable discontinuity, the rupture, between past and present. Equally, however, Godfrey's claim could be taken up in a mood of pathos in which the partial success in achieving relations between past and present motivates one to test to what degree such relations have been achieved, how they endure, how and when they break down, and what are the technologies of repair available for the artist at a particular time.

Godfrey's fourth topic: the goal of painting is to seek to render things visible that are "unknowable and un-representable."[35] Godfrey is not arguing that painting is impossible or thoroughly imaginary, in the sense of subjective or psychological. Rather, he means that there are domains whose being cannot be captured through discourse (*énoncés*), whether it be direct or indirect. Such domains, furthermore, are not things or images or forms that can be captured through drawing representational attention to a referent. The challenge of art is to attain the register of visibility qua visibility.

One consistent technique that Richter employs to ward off direct representation is to confront it head on and to interfere with it. Thus, his numerous paintings of clouds or seascapes (or for that matter cities) incite an initial representational response in the observer, which is then undercut, disaggregated, reduced, or disrupted so as to make visible, among other things, the materiality of the paint, the collage effects underlying what had seemed initially to be realistic, and the diverse visibilities available depending on how close or how far one stands in viewing. Such techniques oblige an acknowledgment of how things are known and seen. How do aesthetic objects come into being?

Godfrey's final topic: "how could the practice of painting continue without subjective content?"[36] To the degree that Godfrey is correct in assessing Richter as accepting and experimenting with solutions to this problem, then, once again, those critics who interpret Richter's paintings in terms of intentionality, their subjective content, for either the painter or the viewer, are themselves falling into the fallacy of taking up painting as the object of an inquiry or a symptom of the painter or the epoch.

Imagery

Godfrey closes the first part of his lecture by wondering, "What if Richter's approach to the natural is inseparable from his approach to history?" Godfrey begins to answer his rhetorical question in what follows. He asks,

"Where did this brutal image of nature come from?" His answer: the Nazi extermination camps. The camps were set in the German and Polish countryside. Godfrey shows opening clips from Alain Resnais's *Night and Fog* and Claude Lansmann's *Shoah*, the two greatest cinematic attempts to confront the Holocaust. In both, there is an idyllic image of the countryside, befitting the modernist contempt for the evocation of traditional landscape painting. Thereafter, remaining remnants of the pastoral are shattered.

Of the remarkably rare photographic images of the extermination camps during their time of gruesome operation, a blank hole in the twentieth century's ever-expanding avalanche of images, there is one of a copse of birch trees outside of the eponymously named Birkenau camp. Godfrey refers to "a curtain of trees" around the camp.[37]

One existing photo of special significance is blurred (presumably hurriedly taken from the hip) and is grayish in tone. Didi-Huberman draws an analogy between the gray of the photograph and the gray of the cinders, remains of those cremated in the furnaces. Richter himself, along with the critical literature following his lead, has given much attention to his use of gray. Among other qualities, Richter has periodically in his career (and life) praised gray for its meaninglessness and its neutrality.

Godfrey then turns in his lecture to Richter's *Atlas* in which concentration camp photos were first assembled and displayed by the artist. They were placed adjacent to ordinary pornographic images from German magazines of the time (1950s). Richter was contemplating exhibiting both types of images together but decided against it at the last minute. Again, much critical commentary takes up these images in the *Atlas*. Although he backed away from a public exhibition, Richter did return to the photos of the camps. He decided to color parts of the black-and-white photos by tinting a few areas, a gesture that he has not explained. Godfrey offers a compelling interpretation: following an insight from Jean-Francois Lyotard that *"once fixed, memories can be forgotten."* Hence the tinting can be seen plausibly as an immediate gesture of de-familiarization, blocking or interfering with the affective mood of viewing these by now familiar if still terrible photos. Furthermore, the tinting can be seen plausibly as a marking that blocks or defers the images from becoming a memorial.

Godfrey concludes that for Richter, Nature is bound up with these images of the curtain of trees, the forest, the landscape, and the cultivated fields that form the frame for the camps. This unsettling connection is especially true for Birkenau.

There is a photo of this "forest of birches" on the wall in Richter's studio (it also appears in the film). The photo was taken from some distance away. In it one can see several figures who appear to be tending to nature, perhaps cleaning up leaves; they appear at first glance, Richter observes to Serota in another interview, as if they were "nice gardeners." That first impression turns out to be an appalling mistake, perhaps a residue of our habituation to impressionist and post-impressionist views of landscapes or the ever-present snapshots of the countryside. In fact, the photo is an image of *Sonderkommando* burying corpses.

For Richter, the forests, rivers, and fields are haunted by what must be oxymoronically named *Nachleben*, survivals of death in all their brutality, and inhumanity. Godfrey ends his lecture by turning to a series of twelve paintings Richter undertook in 1990 with the series title of *Wald* (*Forest*). These are paintings of darkness and concealment. He concludes that the forest or woods that once stood for a protected space, a sanctuary, and a home can no longer retain such a univocal meaning any more than those meanings left over from the Romantics.

"The woods are a very different place now."

Mean, Excess, Deficiency

The English language translator of Didi-Huberman's book underscores the polysemy of the French word *tout* in the title of the book. He explains:

> The single French word *tout* can be translated into English variously as "all," "whole," "every," "any"—words which in English, contrary to the French, vary distinctively in meaning, laying out problems for translation. Since the word *tout* refers to a crucial concept in the text, I believe it is important to follow the author and to keep to one word "all" in most instances—even where the choice (as it is in the French text) is syntactically unusual.[38]

The terms "spite" and "despite" could both have been used to translate the French term "*malgré*" in the title of Didi-Huberman's book. It seems to me that "despite" would have been a better translation than "spite." Either way,

I add a third term "respite" to expand and thereby complete the series. This term is implied in Didi-Huberman's book and in his defense of his public use of unique images of the extermination camps (first in an exhibition in Paris and then in his book). Although the term *respite* does not appear in the raging debates Didi-Huberman found himself involved with over the ethics of showing such images at all, the term hangs over the discussion. The question: does making these singular images of terrible events available in any way mitigate, afford comfort, allow respite, diminish the pressure, or free us from the burden of the revulsion at what is portrayed?

> Respite: relieve (v.)
> late 14c., "alleviate (pain, etc.), mitigate; afford comfort; allow respite; diminish the pressure of," also "give alms to, provide for"; also figuratively, "take heart, cheer up"; from Old French *relever* "to raise, relieve" (11c.) and directly from Latin *relevare* "to raise, alleviate, lift up, free from a burden," from *re-*, intensive prefix (see *re-*), + *levare* "to lift up, lighten," from *levis* "not heavy" (see *lever*).[39]

As a means of approaching the problem of the motion and mode despite it all, Didi-Huberman presents a series of markers for establishing excess and deficiency in taking up this problem. His approach is invigorating because it provides an observation point for lessons learned derived from his vast scholarly work. It is even more invigorating in that it does not assume the mean is easily attainable or even nameable.

Didi-Huberman presents poles of excess or deficiency (although he does not specify which is which and presumably either pole could function in either way). His first claim is that the "language of the unimaginable" can go wrong in two ways (which he calls modes).

One pole is *aestheticism*, which errs by missing the concrete singularity of that which one is trying to comprehend, think, image.

The corresponding pole is *historicism*, which errs by missing the formal specificity of the object or situation or mood.[40]

His second series of markers turns on two ways of being inattentive.[41]

The one pole (and here this applies primarily to images) is called *hypertrophy* or wanting to show everything. Pushing too hard in this direction makes an image into an icon.

The second consists in *desiccating* the image, thereby making it into a document. By so doing an interpretation of an image risks appearing more informative, more objective, than it actually is in reality.

> *Images in spite of all*, which calls for a difficult ethics of the image: neither the invisible par excellence (the laziness of the aesthete), nor the icon of horror (the laziness of the believer), nor the mere document (the laziness of the learned). A simple image: inadequate but necessary, inexact but true.[42]

9/11: Deficient or Excessive?

However ineptly—desperately ineptly—I set about it, my will, my endeavor, my effort—what drives me—is the quest for enlightenment (apprehension of "truth," and of the interconnections; coming closer to a meaning; so all my pessimistic, nihilistic actions and assertions have the sole aim of creating or discovering hope).
—Gerhard Richter[43]

In 2005, Richter produced a single painting of one of the airliners approaching an already burning World Trade Center tower. Robert Storr, who had written an earlier scholarly book on Richter's work as well as one on the October 1977 paintings, which, as we have seen, he brought to the Museum of Modern Art in New York. The book is somewhat deceptively entitled *September: A History Painting by Gerhard Richter*.[44] I say deceptively because the book is as much about the events of 9/11 as about the painting per se. It is not clear that the history presented has much if anything to do with the painting itself.

Storr was living in New York at the time of the attacks, and he opens and ultimately frames the book with an awkward personal account (one-fourth of the small book). His narration of what he felt and his concerns over his daughters' well-being in Brooklyn, while no doubt sincere, have nothing directly to do with Richter or the painting. Additionally, Storr includes many of the standard, and extremely well-known, press photographs of the event. He includes a series of journalistic photographs of other events (e.g., assassination in Vietnam) that he contributes as if it were self-evident that they are part of the same history. By doing so, he never confronts the problem of whether he was producing history or genealogy and what either has to do with painting today.

Yet, once again, Richter must have acquiesced to having the diverse photographs and Storr's autobiographical meanderings included in the book. This personalization and this array of representational imagery precisely cut against the grain of everything Richter argues for and against in his comments on *War Cut*—as we shall see below. Of equal consequence, Storr's interpretation violates a number of the critical parameters outlined in the previous section.

We are told that Richter and his wife were flying to New York for an opening of an exhibition of his work at the Marian Goodman Gallery when their plane was diverted to Nova Scotia. The couple returned to Germany two days later. This minor inconvenience hardly explains why Richter would have chosen to attempt to produce a painting ostensibly about "the event."

Referring to the attackers, Storr quotes Richter as observing that having such an overriding ideological motivation can produce "tremendous strength, the terrifying power that an idea has which goes as far as death. That is the impressive thing to me, and the most inexplicable thing; that we produce ideas, which are almost not only almost utterly wrong and nonsensical but above all dangerous."[45] And yet, as with *War Cut*, compelling ideas generated in reaction to abominable events can themselves produce dangerous effects and affects.

It is only in chapter 4 of Storr's book that the painting finally is examined. Atypically for Richter, the painting consists of only two layers. Further, for whatever reasons, paint was scraped off with a knife rather than the squeegee, Richter's signature technique. Using the knife, Richter removed a thin layer of paint right down to the canvas. This scraping highlighted the prominence of the image of the plane and towers in the center of the small canvas.[46] Once again, this simplicity runs against the grain of Richter's usual manner of proceeding, in which the initial image is transformed multiple times. Here, Storr writes:

> The image is faintly perceptible in the contrasting greys that dominate the canvas and in the faint blush of color that grows stronger as the viewer approaches, allowing the eye to acclimate to the dim light that imbues the picture, for despite first appearances, it is a picture and not one of Richter's monochrome abstractions, a *Bild* and not an *Abstraktes Bild*.[47]

Storr recounts that Richter was demoralized by the early versions of the work, which he saw as having failed to escape from the representational. Richter told a reporter in 2005 that he intended to destroy the painting. However, he did not. By doing so, Richter allowed the painting to be interpreted in *historicist* terms. Then again, perhaps that was the way it was painted.

A Memorial, Not a Contemporary Image?

Hubertus Butin also has a positive interpretation of Richter's 9/11 painting. "I think he has succeeded in creating a memorial against terrorism, against ideological fanaticism."[48]

He judges the painting to be successful and moving because of its avoidance of direct representation of the plane crashing into one of the twin towers, although that image is actually rather prominent. For Butin, the way in which Richter avoids realism is through the use of his famous and branded technique, the squeegee (Storr's assertion that Richter used a knife notwithstanding). Over the figurative representation of one of the twin towers, Richter deploys his squeegee to scrape and move the paint across the surface of the canvas so as to partially obscure the underlying representation. In that manner, the critic claims the viewer is provided with a distance in order to reflect on the event's meaning and thereby to remain loyal to Richter's oft-pronounced desire to remain free of ideological constraints of any sort.

Here, in my opinion, Richter's interference work (and the critic's reaction to it) does not work very well at all. First, there is basically no *Nachleben* acknowledged either in the painting or in the event although Storr does make an attempt to move in that direction. Second, the technique of the squeegee was by that stage in his career one of Richter's well-known trademarks and in and of itself did not disrupt the spectator's expectations; rather, it reminded seasoned viewers of how many ways Richter had deployed the technique elsewhere to richer ends. Further, Storr claims Richter was using a knife and not a squeegee, although the point that Butin is making would remain the same either way. Thus, the interference technique in this instance did not succeed in disrupting either the representational or the affective reality. Richter's 9/11 painting, I observe sarcastically but not ironically, would work rather well on a tee shirt.

Butin's admiration turns on the following quote: "Richter has created a distance between painter and viewer. In so doing, the depicted event becomes a subject of reflection."

In sum, I think that the fixed relation that Butin claims Richter is providing between the observer and the image in his 9/11 painting may well be there. To the degree they are achieved, however, is the degree, I argue, that the painting is not successful. To the degree that Richter's image (*Bild*) activates or motivates or induces a *Bildung* of reflection on terrorism and ideological fanaticism is the degree to which the painting becomes an illustration.

Memorial or Inattentive?

As concerns Butin's other claim—that Richter has succeeded in the 9/11 painting in creating "a memorial against terrorism and against ideological fanaticism"—Mark Godfrey makes a compelling case that the very power, richness, and originality of Richter's images, when they "work," consist in his vigilant negative anticipation of images that might be taken as memorials. Consequently, to the extent that Richter's 9/11 painting (and the preparatory sketches) functions as an explicit memorial, it is a failure.

By becoming an illustration, it falls into Didi-Huberman's category of the *inattentive* and the parameter of the *desiccating*. "*Desiccating* the image thereby making it into a document. By so doing an interpretation of an image risks appearing more informative, more objective, that it actually is in reality."

In my opinion, Richter rarely fails in this manner. *September* is, however, not the only instance in which he has done so. Richter is neither providing any identifiable space for the viewer to comfortably occupy nor opening a stable and recognizable space for reflection. Consequently, Richter was perhaps, alas, indeed producing a memorial and depicting an event so as to make it a subject of reflection for viewers.

To quote Richter:

> The motive or rather the premise of my new pictures is the same as that of almost all my other pictures: it is that I can communicate nothing, that there is nothing to communicate, that painting can never be communication, that neither hard work, obstinacy, lunacy nor any trick whatsoever is going to make the absent message emerge of its own accord from the painting process. I don't paint for the sake of painting.[49]

A Painter of Actuality?

In a famous passage, Charles Baudelaire characterized what he called the "painter of modern life" as follows:

But evening comes. . . . Good men and bad turn their thoughts to pleasure, and each hurries to his favourite haunt to drink the cup of oblivion. M. Guys will be the last to leave any place where the departing glories of daylight linger, where poetry echoes, life pulsates, music sounds; any place where a human passion offers a subject to his eye where natural man and conventional man reveal themselves in strange beauty, where the rays of the dying sun play on the fleeting pleasure of the "depraved animal!" . . . Few men have the gift of seeing; fewer still have the power to express themselves. And now, whilst others are sleeping, this man is leaning over his table, his steady gaze on a sheet of paper, exactly the same gaze as he directed just now at the things about him, brandishing his pencil, his pen, his brush, splashing water from the glass up to the ceiling, wiping his pen on his shirt, hurried, vigorous, active, as though he was afraid the images might escape him, quarrelsome though alone, and driving himself relentlessly on. And things seen are born again on the paper, natural and more than natural, beautiful and better than beautiful, strange and endowed with an enthusiastic life, like the soul of their creator. The weird pageant has been distilled from nature. All the materials, stored higgledy-piggledy by memory, are classified, ordered, harmonized, and undergo that deliberate idealization, which is the product of a childlike perceptiveness, in other words a perceptiveness that is acute and magical by its very ingenuousness."[50]

Walking or quickening his pace, he goes his way, forever in search but of what?

Contemporary: Images of the Actual

Art as part of our insane capacity for hope makes it possible that we cope with our permanent madness and our boundless brutality.
—Gerhard Richter

Richter's hesitation over the decades about how to render visible something about the Holocaust is one side of a case; perhaps it is a limit.[51] His patient willingness to render visible something about later events in Germany—Baader-Meinhof and the fall of the Berlin Wall—can be seen both as a part of a larger undertaking as well as having their own episodic characteristics.

Perhaps they can be seen as different approaches to the "permanent madness and our boundless brutality" as Richter puts it.

Gerhard Richter is not Constantine Guys, Baudelaire's painter of modern life. He is a contemporary image-maker: but of what? He is immersed in the present but always in the midst of a swirling tide pool of images. For periods, and at times, the images that immerse him are photographs, either his own or those of others. This modern status of the maker of photographs as privileged is not one Richter accepts: he is not an art photographer or a photojournalist. Rather, it is the work on the images that has been and to an extent continues to be present to Richter. The images and the technologies that produce the images are of interest as first-order technē that he will redouble or cancel or transform. Thus, for example, the repetitive patterns of computer-generated strips of color that Richter has reworked can be taken as an instance of different technē serving as yet another experiment in producing series and/or variations.

Richter is restive. His restiveness is not aimed directly at representations; or perhaps more accurately, his materials are frequently but never uniquely representational. Perhaps here is where an ethos of perseverance or pursuit until something satisfying is obtained begins to appear. What "something satisfying" means is never expanded on by Richter; his work is an incessant effort to make something appear.

These "somethings," however, are not simply or directly the product of the artist's imagination. They are already mediated in multiple ways. Is Richter making artifacts that are elements in a broader configuration of actuality? Is Richter making artifacts that are elements in a configuration to come? Is making in a contemporary mode a means of deploying obstinacy to the modern configurations of the actual? Is Richter's *Haltung* a recalcitrant one insofar as he refuses to engage directly with existing configurations of the actual—but attempts to remain adjacent to them?

It seems to me that the invention of the Readymade was the invention of reality. It was the crucial discovery that what counts is reality, not any worldview whatever. Since then, painting has never represented reality; it has *been* reality (creating itself). And sooner or later the value of this reality will have to be denied, in order (as usual) to set up pictures [images?] of a better world.[52]

Contemporary

In a contemporary mode: what is a reflective relation to the present? Perhaps with Kluge and Richter it is rendering present the present. It is a form of not making it meaningful in a narrative sense. It is a kind of worked-over snapshot that cannot be mistaken as either spontaneous or representational. There always seems to be a reason or a perspective as to why one is rendering a scene or offering some words of description as worth presenting. Although they are already once removed from immediate experience (a photo or a self-conscious description), they double back to present something that seems like it has a quality of immediacy without a defining context.

It is the defining context however that arises with configurations of the actual. So the technē is a kind of second-order reversal: a drawing out of the actual and re-rendering an instant or a moment of perhaps even an instance (perhaps not) as a dimension of the reflective relation to the present.

Such a technē is contemporary in that it is a stylization based on awareness that representation and construction are not the best way to proceed. The reflective relation to the present in a contemporary mode today must take back the narrative and imagistic frames.

Hence there is a strange kind of bracketing. It is in strong opposition to Husserl's bracketing (*epoché*) that was designed to get us to "the things themselves." Rather it is a reversal of Weber's directionality or at least a re-iteration: knowing that the actual interconnection of things is a lure as well as a mirage and that only the interconnection of concepts can have the hope of establishing a significant new point of view—contemporary work seems to entail passing through Weber's connections and then to travel backwards through its steps in a second-order, adjacent manner.

I look for the object and the picture; not for painting or the picture of painting, but for our picture, our books and appearances and views, definitive and total. How shall I put it: I want to picture to myself what is going on now. Painting can help us in this, and the different methods=subjects=themes are the different attempts I make in this direction. Seen in this way, the subject of the picture in the photographic pictures, for instance, is as it is, just as flat, imprecise and superficial; in the Doors and so on, it's symbolic kitsch; in the Details its decoration; in the Landscapes its retrospective, nothing has changed; in the Grey picture it is lack of differentiation, nothing, nil, the beginning and the end; in the Panes of Glass it is the analogy with attitudes and possibilities; in the Color Charts it is chance; anything is correct, or rather Form is Nonsense; in the new Abstract Paintings it is arbitrariness, almost anything is possible.

To me, this arbitrariness has always seemed the central problem in both abstract and representational painting. What reason is there, other than some stupid system or the rules of the game, for placing one thing next to another in any particular format, any particular color, with any particular outline, with any particular likeness—and next to that something else again, no matter what—(a problem I have already touched on).

Firstly, as I have said, pure painting—if it could ever exist—would be a crime; and secondly, these pictures are valued solely and uniquely for their stupid, bumptious, object content. This naturally includes the effective recording of the painter's blind, ferocious motor impulse, as well as the maintaining of a semblance of intelligent and historical awareness through the choice and invention of a motif.

These painters of spontaneity take Cage's saying, which is so important to me, "I have nothing to say, and I am saying it," and they twist it round into "we have nothing to say and we are *not* saying it." Thus they mask and cover up their own impotence, helplessness, and sheer stupidity, with stage sets and fashionably nostalgic debris from the rubbish heap of history. Nazis in disguise.[53]

Object: 1989

We have recently lived through the murders of Charlie Hebdo. These murders demand a requiem, for modernity must be able to respond. But we have to rely on a Requiem by Mozart or Brahms, because the majority of modern music lacks the capacity for grief.
—Alexander Kluge

Art has always been about agony, desperation and helplessness. (I am thinking about the Crucifixion narratives, from the Middle Ages to Grünewald, but also of Renaissance portraits, Mondrian and Rembrandt, Donatello and Pollack.) We often neglect this side of things by concentrating on the formal aesthetic side in isolation. We no longer see content in form . . . the fact is that content does not

have a form (like a dress you can change); it is form (which cannot be changed). Agony, desperation and helplessness cannot be presented except aesthetically, because their source is the wounding of beauty (perfection).
—Gerhard Richter

The quotation from Richter given above concerns his paintings *November*, *December*, and *January*. The quote was elicited by Storr so as to compare *September* with three canvases painted in 1989 at the time of the fall of the Berlin wall (9 November 1989 and the months following).[54]

Richter's former assistant Dieter Schwarz wonders: what is the problem that this practice [of a series] addresses? Schwarz argues that this practice differs from cycles of paintings in which formal variations of aspects of a motif provide the organizing principle. Schwarz gives the example of: "The three winter paintings *November*, *December*, and *January* come closest to forming a cycle, their titles evoking the passage of time and, in metaphorical terms, transience."[55] It may well be that Richter agreed—once again—to have these three paintings called a cycle.

In my view, however, the interpretation Schwarz provides of these paintings is contestable. If these paintings were intended as a cycle of months in a season, then they would be repeated each year. Richter could then be plausibly seen as making a claim about the seasons or perhaps about the affect of coming winter. They might well have been uptakes of the older genre of calendar stories. Richter did experiment with that tradition in his first book with Alexander Kluge: *December*. Such an interpretation in this case, however, would be *aestheticist*, to use Didi-Huberman's vocabulary: "*Aestheticism* that errs by missing the concrete singularity of that which one is trying to comprehend, think, image." As we shall see, there is a concrete singularity to these paintings. It is however not oriented either to a memorial remembrance or to establishing a fixed viewing distance that would create a relationship between the audience and the paintings. There is no message of either sort: "The 'messages' and therefore the content. (Almost) always when painters 'communicate,' they illustrate and give visual expression to their own stupidity. Their messages are always distressing, boring, untruthful, botched, abject and aggressive."[56] It is hard to disagree.

The paintings under consideration were produced in 1989: the Berlin Wall came down on 9 November 1989. There are a number of other indications, including statements by Richter (see below) that the paintings were connected to, or arose during, what were taken by so many others as constituting self-evidently fateful events. Strikingly, the somber mood of Richter's paintings stands in stark contrast to the joy and celebrations that broke out, especially in West Germany.

It seems to me that these paintings are not a cycle but a distinctive *ensemble* that is not going to be repeated. There is an arrow of time whose meaning will only be determined in the future. Richter was clearly not filled with joy. We can conclude that he sees the triumph of consumer capitalism and democracy not as an entirely favorable and irreversible turning point instantiating liberation but rather as the third leg after the rise and fall of communism and fascism — although distinctive and posing different challenges and dangers — of the long and dreadful twentieth century.

There is no doubt that the two ideological boundary markers for Richter were the Communist regime in the GDR and the Nationalist Socialist one in *Deutschland*. The status of consumer capitalism as the available alternative to both claimed Richter's attention and that of his friends in the art world during the 1960s (as we saw in the chapter on his collaborations with Sigmar Polke and Blinky Palermo). Given Richter's return in the 1980s to the problem of images in spite of all, we can tentatively assume that for him the advent of consumer capitalism is an event in a longer series with no defined future horizon.

Lament

The ensemble *November, December,* and *January,* it seems to me, is an attempt at a contemporary lament. These paintings have received less critical attention than many others in Richter's vast oeuvre, no doubt in part because they are not figurative or ostensibly referential and in part because their affect runs against the grain of the reigning *doxa*.

Storr describes the artist's mood in 1989 as follows:

They are three diptychs *November, December,* and *January,* the months following October. It is, as if, after a hiatus, Richter had shifted gears aesthetically to record the rising anguish of the "German Autumn" of 1977 as it passed into a long dark winter of discontent. Heavily encrusted with black anthracite and cold white pigment that has been raked over so that in spots reds and yellows crackle like embers, these raw but masterful canvases suck up all the oxygen in the room they occupy and occlude any view of the world beyond. Punctuating a decade that began with painterly fireworks and heralding a generally harsher variety of overall abstraction, these paintings are a coda to *October 18, 1977*, a majestic dirge for a bitter era.[57]

The limitation of this judgment is that it is epochal. It identifies a decade as a significant unit (plausible perhaps historically). It identifies this decade as a *kairos*, not an event in a longer series that ramifies from a prior turning point. It places Richter as reactive to that period.

In sum, it portrays Richter as a painter of the age of the world picture. It portrays Richter as a Romantic expressionist. It portrays Richter as a failed modern in his refusal to "make it new." Perhaps Storr is giving us an example of why theory is dangerous. In any case, his interpretation qualifies for Didi-Huberman's category of the *inattentive*.

In a note dated 10 November 1989, Richter wrote:

> The events in the GDR, the so-called historic, democratic revolution. Moved though I am by it, in spite of the briefly flaring hopes of a happy future, a reunited Germany, I am overwhelmed by skepticism and pessimism, almost grief, sometimes rage. Rage at the shamelessly opportunistic politicians, and at the intellectuals who spouted for decades in their fanatical Marxist blindness and now sulk, unable to let go of their conceit of knowing better. Grief at the role assigned to the people, who have been systematically used—casually cooped up like convicts for 40 years, by those who would be quite happy to keep them there for another 140— and now used in a different way and persuaded that they have created this democratic revolution themselves, by their own efforts. When it is perfectly plain that they are being sent out through the [Berlin] wall and allowed into the West.[58]

Richter's anger and grief give one pause. One can interpret him as saying that what everyone considers to be a *kairos* is actually an event—an event in a series? It is an event that continues a line of blindness, arrogance, and enclosure. Is that the *ensemble*? Is it an attempt to produce a moving ratio when others see an epochal change?

4

COMPOSITION *Technē* and Pathos

Technē 1: Gerhard Richter's Pathos

Our expressive gestures are perhaps limited, or if they are not, they are strongly conditioned by our cultural atavism. Thus the plunge into technique can be liberating and can make it possible to discover expressive gestures for which we were not prepared.

When we are in the process of writing a work, we are at one and the same time in a state of research and of reference: Reference, not only in relation to the historical material but also in relation to ourselves, to our own past. Thus there is a reprise of certain paths, even certain obsessions; our sensibility must learn new things while knowing that we may not know how to approach them. Despite our desire to project into the future, it is the immediate (or far-off) past that we are putting into question.

—Pierre Boulez

It is very hard for a German not to be tragic. It is equally hard for a German not to fall back on a sulky irony if the tragic is beyond one's skills or the genre in which one labors. One of Gerhard Richter's most distinctive achievements, one apparently not schematized by the ever-growing number of scholars treating his work and his life, is at the deepest level his *manner* of painting—with its pale assonances with his life—resulting in his pathos.

Although *pathos* is an old term, appearing, for example, in Aristotle's *Rhetoric*, and although it has had a long and varied history, in modernity it finds its places in the realms of theater and medicine.[1] The dictionary definitions of *pathos* equate it with a form of emotion. In our understanding, this equation is not only incorrect but also misleading. Pathos is an affect term; it is a structured milieu in which emotions and representations qualify and are shaped within specific forms. Affect is not an emotion in that it is a relational state and not an interior one; affect does not emanate from the subject as the sentimental novels and literature of the eighteenth century represented emotion.[2]

This relational structure of affect is one reason that the theater was a privileged site of experimentation and experience for a long time. The pathos of pathology in medicine takes place in the doctor-patient scene in which bodily materiality, suffering, and attempts to understand and compensate for disease, suffering, and finitude take their place.[3]

Of course, there are many different kinds of affect; they can be given many different forms. Among four moods (pathos, tragedy, irony, and comedy), Richter's work is cast distinctively and pervasively in a mood of pathos. Furthermore, to complicate the narrative one more turn, while it is certainly contestable that Richter's work could be narrated otherwise than in the form we are giving it, on a second-order level of experience, experimentation, and narrative, we ourselves are self-consciously organizing the material under consideration in a mood of pathos. It follows that the relation of our narrative mood and other interpretations of Richter, by critics or the artist himself, might well be ironic, comic, or in a mood of pathos — so be it.

The manner in which I am taking up Richter's work is what I intend as a contemporary one. The problem and the challenge is this: given a mood of pathos, how to proceed so as to make one's practice an exercise, an experiment, and a test. In order to make a plausible demonstration of these variables I will have to examine the themes of *technē*, of mood, of mode of subjectivation, and of Richter's paintings' capacity to make visible a *Bild* with a reality-effect. Such reality-effects make no claim, visually or otherwise, to be totalizing, symbolic, synecdochic, or analogical world pictures. Nor are they a continuation of the unstable relation of painter and subject under the regime of sovereignty. Yet, Richter's overall oeuvre, if not every instance, does carry forward that problem if not the solution. Here is an example, among others, of *Nachleben* and of *Pathosformel*.

Interferences

Hubertus Butin, curator of a major exhibit of Richter's *Editions* in Berlin in 2011, in his video presentation on the Richter website (and in his published writings) poses the following question as being at the heart of Richter's work: what is an image today?[4]

It is a commonplace to assert that the image currently finds itself in a troubled location between the history of images (art, photography, etc.) and the current global saturation of omnipresent media obtainable at an unprecedented scale and scope. Butin describes Richter as incessantly testing multiple possibilities in order to discover passages through this media-saturated topology as well as the spectral historical archive. This characterization can serve as a crisp identification as well as a diagnosis of a contemporary problem-space. In order to achieve and maintain a contemporary mood, the artist and critics, as well as observers, must acknowledge the dynamics of this mutually interfering and enhancing activity and attempt to find a form of addressing it by taking it up as an experience, a milieu, a technical challenge, and a test.

Translated into my terms, an initial formulation of the problem-space highlights the problem of the presence of *Nachleben* in a modern space, and what to make of them in terms of form and significance. In that light, the working and reworking, as well as accepting and rejecting, with multiple possible forms constitute the realm of the *Pathosformel*. Finally, as we shall see, in order to complete the series of the parameters of the contemporary, I identify a distinguishing *kairos* for Gerhard Richter that occasions much of his image-making in both direct and oblique ways.

From the Technical to Technē: Moiré

Following established critical conventions, Butin argues that Richter's highly diverse artistic output has been consistently mediated by the use of a range of industrial techniques. Fundamentally, Richter establishes transactions with the world of images by acknowledging the centrality of industrial technique in their production, reproduction, and dissemination. In that sense, Richter has affirmed, albeit with a bittersweet tone, Marcel Duchamp's famous claim that painting was over but that one needed nonetheless to continue making art. In Richter's case, he has restively pursued a practice of painting that is neither nostalgic nor avant-garde. Indeed, how to find a mean, if that is what it is, constitutes an ongoing challenge for him. Experimenting, checking, and evaluating the forms he restlessly produces organize, I argue, a test not only for the daily practice of the artist but for critics and observers as well.

Throughout his career, Richter has been resolutely antimodernist, if by that one understands the modernist commitment to consist in the motivation to show the inherent worth of rendering painting as nothing but painting through finding means to show that the materials and their arrangement on a canvas refer to themselves and themselves alone. It is not that Richter totally rejects the high modernist striving for abstraction and rupture as historical conditions, but he takes up abstraction and rupture not as goals in and of themselves but as available techniques and thereby sees his challenge as finding ways to make them function differently. These premises and practices of high modernism in the arts are by now not so much obliterated or irrelevant for Richter but part of a moving ratio with the near future.

As an example of this refunctioning attitude and practice, Butin picks out *moiré*. *Moiré* refers to a mistake that occurs in the printing process resulting in a blurring or an inconsistency in the printed-out image. Richter takes up the effect produced by a technical imperfection, abstracts it from the norms that classify it as an error, and instead lets it stand as a technical procedure that could be used to produce distinctive image-effects.

Another example of this opportunistic and transformative approach concerns color. For Richter, gray is the absence of color; hence it is the tone best suited to escape or at least reduce referentiality and meaning.[5] Again, he refuses to take up gray in a high modernist mode in which the purported purity and self-referentiality of the color become its connotation, as in Yves Klein's use of blue as both transcendental in and of itself and as simultaneously the artist's avant-garde signature. Richter is fully aware of Malevich's color squares and their claim to purity as well as the twentieth-century tradition of such monochrome canvasses that followed these early breakthroughs and ruptures, leading, for example, to the work of a painter like Robert Ryman, whose white or nearly white canvasses continue that mode and for whom Richter expresses some admiration. Richter's test has been to acknowledge and accept the place of this tradition and then to interfere with its use of color as an end in itself. Rather, he subsequently strives to formulate and put into practice a response to the challenge of what kinds of techniques constitute high modernism, how they can be disaggregated—and how, thereby, they can become available to redefine the artist's *technē* as a site of production and experience.

Butin illustrates the general points about technique, color, and Richter's "aesthetic of absence" through the example of Richter's famous painting of his daughter Betty, her blond hair and red-and-white robe vividly foregrounded. This seemingly realistic portrait has received multiple critical interpretations. These range from blunt criticism of the painting as sentimental and commercial to a sophisticated interpretation of the figure of Betty, who we see with her head turned away, as really an instantiation of Walter Benjamin's famous evocation of Paul Klee's *Angelus Novus*, which Benjamin narrates as looking back toward the storms of history while being blown forward into the future.

Butin, by examining the painting more closely, and no doubt after discussions with Richter, points out that what Betty is portrayed as gazing at is not the history of capitalism, but rather a contrastive gray canvas (whose bottom edge is visible in the painting) in the background. With this arrangement of elements, Richter establishes a relationship between the photorealism of the dominant figure in the foreground and the gray tableau with its presumed lack of meaning or referentiality in the background. Such an internal relationship thereby functions as an interference technique disrupting or disqualifying those looking for direct reference and its associated meaning but equally doing the same for those asserting the impossibility or definitional absence of reference or meaning.

One could say that Richter wants it both ways by having both figural and nonfigural focal points; or one could see the painting as a particularly provocative and successful exemplar of how an insistence on the presence of *Nachleben* can be combined with an assertive realism (techniques learned during his days at the East German Academy no doubt) to produce a *Pathosformel* in which the necessity and futility of this arrangement presses the artist, critic, and spectator into a domain of visibility (and thought) that qualifies as contemporary.

Another example that Butin discusses is Richter's use of color charts. The artist has experimented with them for many years. One of their attractions for Richter is that color charts do not depict anything; they are simply, as it were, an arrangement of the spectrum of color understood as a fact of nature, produced by techniques that have broken free of trade secrets or artistic genius. In that light, a leading art historian of modernism, Rosalind Krauss, has nominated color charts as "an emblem of modernity" because they only appeared in the early twentieth century as part of the industrialization of paint (again, Duchamp comes to mind).

One could say that this aspect of modernism is a *Nachleben* in Richter's present but not one he makes actual in the manner that his modernist predecessors have done. Rather, he sees it as an ordinary thing of the world, open to be taken up in a second-order manner by artist or critic. In response to the ordinariness, Richter does not turn to a craft moment of mixing his own paints and making that craft dimension visible, but rather he takes the colors charts and rearranges the spectrum. The ordering of the industrial paint charts is thereby accepted as an ordinary thing of the world but not its naturalness. The flow through a gradated series from one end of the spectrum to another that one can see in any paint store is taken as a gradated series from what was taken to be one end of the spectrum of visibility for human eyes to the other. In sum, Richter is not taking color to be an industrialized nature; rather, he is taking it as a series of what has been taken to be an industrialized nature so that it can be arranged and rearranged.

What technique does Richter employ in order to render the quality of denaturalized seriality visible? The answer is another technique that clearly fascinates Richter, one he is attracted to and yet, once again, wants to reproblematize—chance. Richter developed a simple technique whereby the serial order could be redistributed; he took the individual color chips, put them in a container and then arbitrarily picked them out one by one and placed them on the chart. Richter, however, did not leave the implementation of his search for such a technique, as it were, to chance or arbitrariness. Rather, once again, he combined chance with planning—systematizing the variations that he had first discovered by this crude method—thereby undermining the modernist reference to the play of chance in and of itself by accepting the modernist gambit but mediating it by introducing technological ordering practices. As a result, the arbitrariness was not fetishized but made visible as a practice, thereby opening it up to further uses and understandings.

A third type of interference that Butin discusses is that of iconography. Richter has experimented over the years with a series of paintings of candles.

Candles were a well-known part of the *Vanitas* genre that flourished in the seventeenth century; there, the closeness of death and the foolishness of worldly pleasures and distractions were brought into view. It would seem to be unproblematic to connect Richter's paintings of candles (and an occasional skull) to the *Vanitas* paintings, and critics have done so, often in a didactic tone.

This pedagogy, however, is misleading. First, Butin points out that several of Richter's paintings are of a single candle, which in and of itself violates the traditional iconographic conventions of always including more than one candle. Consequently, Richter's self-conscious transformation of the canon should be understood, once again, as a technique of interference, lest the viewer or critic assume that Richter's candles have a fixed meaning carried forward through the ages.

That being said, it probably is true that they do have a referent, the *Nachleben* of the *Vanitas* tradition and the specters of the meaning they once had as techniques of moral pedagogy in a world long since gone but not entirely forgotten. It follows that to claim that Richter's choice of depicting candles figuratively is entirely arbitrary is unconvincing; if that were the case, not only would there have been no reason to depict them, but there also would be nothing with which to interfere.

Richter amplifies the iconographical and semantic interference by the different techniques of painting within the image: the candles are painted as mottled, and other parts of the canvas are overpainted with strong black splotches. While it is true, as Butin claims, that such a juxtaposition of seemingly figural and seemingly nonfigural aspects on a single canvas ultimately highlights the materiality of the paint itself, it seems to us that this gesture reaches beyond a modernist gesture priming the visibility and materiality of paint per se to a more complicated interference that retains the candles as survivals or *Nachleben*.

There is a tension here between the ironic and the pathetic. The tension, we hold, may well present a temptation for the critic but not for the artist or the anthropological observer. Why bother undermining or ironizing something long since passed into the past? Why bring it into the frame if not to show that it has an afterlife or survival. If nothing else, it is evocative of the presence of death and our current problems with giving it form, meaning, or significance. Richter's multiple experiments with painting candles can therefore be plausibly seen as experiments in contemporary technique. Such technique is almost certainly not an end in itself but a way of facilitating the recognition of an experience or the lack of a form of something that calls for a *technē*. In other words, the candle paintings might well point to the vanity of certain critics while rendering palpable an affect of the tensions of contemporary experience.

Chance or Indetermination?

A hallmark of a prominent strand of modern painting is its spontaneity, as in the action painting of the New York abstractionists, in which various modes of letting the unconscious be expressed as a means to avoid what were held to be ego structures disposed to block deeper and freer processes, or as in more spiritual attempts to let things happen in a Zen fashion, most closely associated with the thought and performance of John Cage. These approaches were lauded as liberating the artist from the hegemony of the ego and superego or the imagined oppressive figure of Western bourgeois consciousness.

Of these two poles, Richter, as one might expect, had familiarized himself with (and was fascinated by) Cage and his modes of deploying techniques to achieve various de-subjectivizing ends. Equally, as one might expect, Richter experimented with ways to incorporate and reject—or interfere with and redirect—both the techniques themselves and their goals. Richter has taken the techniques initially developed to free the painter's primary processes and reworks those techniques so as to turn them into second-order techniques, ones that interfere with not only primary processes but also with much of modernist painting. Said another way, Richter takes up several of the techniques that arose during key turning points in modern art—various *kairoi*—and de-heroizes them just as he is famous for having done with photography. He is then freer to both retain and transform their effects and their capacities.

Aline Guillermet, in her talk at the Tate for the *Panorama* exhibit, focuses on the theme of chance, uncertainty, and mimesis. She seeks to capture what she sees as the core of Richter's experiments with chance-effects in the aphorism: "Chance representing itself is always representation."[6]

As is well known, throughout his life Richter has kept a vast collection of photos, both his own and those chosen from the mass press. These photos, arranged and rearranged in series, are collected and displayed, presented and redisplayed in the series of publications he has called his *Atlas*. Critics have repeatedly referred to the photos as banal (often in contrast to the noble or the glamorous in the style of Andy Warhol). Perhaps a better term might be "ordinary"; they form a kind of archive, in part intimate in the domestic sense and in part personal in the choices the artist made of which images to preserve among the many available to him.

A selection of these photos has been used in one of Richter's distinctive subgenres: the overpainted photo. It is a subgenre because Richter also has produced overpainted prints and the like. Perhaps the best label overall is overpainted images (*Bilder*). One of the earlier techniques for combining overpainting and chance consisted in Richter selecting a photograph that he then reproduced as a print. The next step was to take large blades to scrape excess paint from the squeegees he used on his canvases. The paint remaining on these scraping blades remained malleable for as long as three days. Richter began experimenting with dripping or smearing the paints remaining on the scrapers onto photo-prints.

Critics have characterized this procedure as one of *chance*. The use of the term *chance* by Richter's art critics turns out to be misleading, however, as its use establishes a series of false dichotomies. For example, Guillermet's talk at the Tate stated as its problem two paradoxes in Richter's overpainted photos. The first was that there was a consistent mimetic effect between the chance overpainting and the photo-prints. How, she wondered, does this harmonization take place if the application of the paint is by chance? The second paradox is how to account for Richter's use of color coordination if such coordination is merely the effect of chance. Both paradoxes, not surprisingly, turn out to not really be paradoxes, as Guillermet proceeds to demonstrate in the remainder of her talk.

Testing

Guillermet draws a distinction between a mechanical approach and one of technical manipulation. The former would presumably be a kind of method that would encompass, in one fashion or another, a wide range of examples and instances. The latter would include a technical mediation of tools and materials that would distance it from craft or the standard of consistent, machine-like regularity. Technical manipulation (or mediation) would neither eliminate the maker's choices, honed by long practice, nor determine the final form or allure of the made.

For Richter, the analog of the chance-effects (or indetermination) that he is seeking to take account of in his own artistic practice is nature. Richter sees in nature the kind of spontaneous, arbitrary, meaningless selection processes that result nonetheless, and to a degree quite unexpectedly, in living forms and beings. Thus, Richter approaches nature in this instance not for its metaphoric value but for its techno-analogic value. What is taking place and how does it work?

Drawing on the book *Chance and Necessity* by the French biologist Jacques Monod, recipient of a Nobel Prize, Guillermet takes Monod's distinction between "essential chance" and "operational chance" and applies it to Richter's procedures and thinking. Essential chance in nature for Monod has to do with the vast recombinatory processes that are not preprogrammed but nevertheless function surprisingly effectively. Monod's example is that of the immune system where unanticipated pairings of antibodies and antigens generally protect the organism despite the fact that these encounters were not programmed prior to their activation. The comparison Guillermet draws with Richter's approach is that he is content to acknowledge that his selection process occurs only at a second-order stage; things happen (paints mix arbitrarily for the given purpose to which they are eventually put, drips drop where they may) but there is directionality to what seems to be essential chance, or primary indetermination.

The second kind of chance for Monod is "operational chance." The example is a roll of the dice or a roulette wheel. If, however, one manipulated the dice before rolling them, then the process would be to a degree under the control of the gamer. Not surprisingly, Guillermet observes that of course Richter knows what colors remain on the blades and therefore chooses the photos accordingly. Consequently, there is no paradox. There is a technical intervention that both establishes and resolves an indeterminate situation without that resolution being mechanically planned beforehand.

In fact, there is no paradox either in the manner in which Richter achieves mimetic effects in his overpainted photo prints; the artist notes the mottled color range left on the blades, chooses a photo that would probably have some assonance with them and then lets the delimited technical intervention take the shape it does. If he likes the result, he keeps it; if he doesn't, he reworks or discards it. In fact, it is precisely because Richter is dealing with indetermination and not chance that his choices, decisions, and artistic *phronesis* come into play.

There is, however, a further level at which a mimetic effect can work. Guillermet shows that when the overpainted photos concern nature (frequently mountainous landscapes), a second affect is introduced. To illustrate her point, she highlights a series of overpainted photos of the high Alps at Sils Maria (where Nietzsche's house now has been turned into a museum). Richter was drawn to the site. Looked at by themselves, the photos of snow-covered mountain scenes in the numerous photos he took there could be read as expressing almost a Romantic sense of the majesty and peace of Nature, especially as the Germans appreciate and appreciated it. Once Richter overpaints them, however, a sense of motion, of disturbance, of an uncovering of another dimension to the mountains is rendered visible precisely through the absolutely non-mimetic, technological intervention of the dripped or smeared paint. This intervention not only disrupts whatever Romantic affect there might have been while marking its presence, its *Nachleben*, but also produces an affect of danger, or nature's inhumanity, its uncontrollability, its foreignness.

Here we must qualify Guillermet's rather comforting claim that "chance representing itself is always representation" with a different and less comforting claim that assembling the *Nachleben*-affect with a radical presence of technical painterly interference produces a second-order sense of indetermination.

Technē 2: Technological Supports + Medium-s + Image

Incited by a decade of disgust at the spectacle of meretricious art called installation . . .
—Rosalind Krauss

Rosalind Krauss, co-founder of *October*, after having suffered a major brain aneurysm, has written a blistering manifesto, saturated with pathos and obstinacy, entitled *Under Blue Cup*, referring to one of the exercises for restoring her memory.[7] The book might well be seen as a kind of all-out defense of modernism in the arts against the decades of postmodernisms, identity politics, and the like, but that would not be quite correct. To the extent that the book and the author are defending a cause, that cause is the specificity of *art*.

In order to do this work, Krauss produces a scathing, sarcastic, and poignant diagnostic attack on the trendy and the dominant in the art world while at the same time providing the lineaments of a diagram of what we would call a *contemporary ethos*. This claim is not entirely an imposition as Krauss does literally provide a diagram, albeit not exactly with a contemporary ethos. In order to grasp what she is after, and how it might be deployed for an adjacent purpose, some preliminary observations are in order.

1st Procedure: Adjacency

As is my practice, I am using the rich work of a respected author, in this instance Krauss, for my own purposes. Those purposes are initially diagnostic and conceptual. I find her diagnosis of the excesses and deficiencies of recent art practice and discourse (and their direct homologies in other fields) telling. That being said, I have no special affective or professional stakes in the expanded and globalized art world or the game of art criticism or expanded curatorial powers as Krauss clearly does—she is "all in," all the time. My analytic reduction and minor larceny of fragments of others' lifework can be defended for what it is—a phase in the practice of assemblage work.

My stakes lie more in the prolonged effort to establish an interpretive adjacency to the work of Gerhard Richter as a singular practitioner of an ethos of the contemporary. Consequently, here, as throughout, I am juxtaposing, and to a lesser degree counterposing, concepts as *Bilder* in a kind of unrequited polyphony with Richter's work and style of creation.

2nd Procedure: Diagnosis

One of the essential externalities of modernism's mandate to "make it new" is that this imperative obliges those who honor it to turn defiantly (or simply destructively, or with unabashed negligence) on the work and accomplishments of their near predecessors. There seem to be no real alternatives to this binary ethos for the avant-garde—short of abandoning the identity altogether, an unthinkable and for many a scandalous alternative. It follows that given the sacrosanct imperative of the new, other targets must be sought. Krauss writes: "The avant-garde was obliged to search for new supports, ones untainted by the stigma of an exhausted tradition."[8] And "Post-Modernism:

the search for an expanded range in part stemming from exhaustion with the modernist insistence on *specificity*."[9] For Krauss this imperative to make it new led in recent decades to excesses of trendiness, media hype, and discursive politics, intertwined with the concurrent vast expansion of consumer markets—all amplified by the maximization of the new media.

Moving assertively forward, vigilantly eschewing nostalgia for the purity of modernism, Krauss insists on alternatives and openings—and identifies artists already exploring available solutions other than the refusal of art per se. For Krauss, the motto now is no longer "make it new" but rather "make it present." To that imperative, we add "in a contemporary mode."

3rd Procedure: Concepts. (a) Technical Supports + (b) Medium-s

With a dogged consistency, the self-styled (self-stymied) avant-garde's first turn in this search for relevance and positionality was to technology, apparently assuming that it constituted the opposite of the traditional, modernist insistence on the purity of the materials. The exploration of technologies as intercessors in the practice and products of art functioned as what Krauss calls "technical supports." She argues that this zealous turn to the primacy of the technological was also a turn against the specificity and ontological significance of art as a category and whose very existence was worth defending.

One might argue, although Krauss does not use this language, that what she saw taking place was a form of active nihilism.

Krauss deploys scathing remarks and underscores her scant regard for this turn of events. Yet she does not leave things at that. Rather, she sees that the expansion of technical supports and the new media contain the potential of turning a mere technical change as a negative and destructive affirmation into the possibility of new *medium-s*.[10]

> It is only the word *medium* that conjures the recursive nature of a successful work of art. The artists who discover the conventions of a new technical support can be said to be "inventing" a medium.
>
> Each of these supports allows the artist to discover its "rules," which will in return become the basis for that recursive self-evidence of a medium's *specificity*. If such artists are "inventing" their medium, they are resisting contemporary art's forgetting of how the medium undergirds the very possibilities of art.

Krauss affirms the work of a number of artists (William Kentridge, Christian Marclay, James Coleman, Sophie Calle, Marcel Broodthaers) who, she argues, have taken the new technological supports that had become so prominent and turned them into medium-s. As I have insufficient familiarity with these artists, I lack the competence to pass judgment on Krauss's judgment. Instead, a petty larcenist from afar, I will juxtapose her concepts to some of Richter's experiments.

(c) Fortuna

Krauss is drawn to the manner in which Kentridge works; this curiosity is facilitated by the fact that Kentridge is observant but not overly theoretical about his own practices. Drawing on one of Kentridge's lectures, "Fortuna: Neither Program nor Chance in the Making of Images," she observes, "Fortuna is Kentridge's word for chance and the luck of seizing it rather than letting it go."[11] To use our technical vocabulary: one of Kentridge's ready-at-hand toolkits is to seize (*lepsis*) a propitious occasion or turn of events that presents itself to the prepared practitioner.

Feeling himself blocked in a drawing he was working on, Kentridge wandered around his studio and suddenly discovered an opening. He observes:

> The sensation was more of discovery than invention. There was no feeling of what a good idea I had had, rather, relief at not having overlooked what was in front of me.
>
> It is only when physically engaged in drawing that ideas start to emerge. There is a combination between drawing and seeing, between making and assessing that provokes a part of my mind that otherwise is closed off.[12]

Thinking as well as creating is a practice.

4th Procedure: Diagram: "The Medium Is the Memory"

Krauss takes up, modifies, and discards Marshall McLuhan's famous aphorism—"the medium is the message"—and repurposes it as "the medium is the memory." Painting is not a message; it has no message. Or, to follow Gilles Deleuze once again, art is not about communication. It is the creation of forms and blocs of sensation that it renders visible. Art criticism observes that work and analyzes how it proceeds, succeeds, or stumbles as well as what it produces.

For Krauss, and I follow her concise and precise formulation here, "The medium is the memory insists on the power of the medium to hold the efforts of the forebears of a specific genre in reserve for the present." The "efforts of the forebears" that need to be attended to are the *Nachleben*. "Forgetting this reserve is the antagonism of memory. The paradigm of the /medium/ could thus be mapped as *memory versus forgetting*."[13] Krauss's formulation implies the obligation to be attentive to *Nachleben* and to the seeming inevitability of the *Pathosformel*.

Efforts at creation whose allegiance to invention moves in this direction are most likely to be cast within an affect of pathos. Why pathos? Probably because of an inherent incompleteness that, should it ever be completed, would turn into exhaustion or kitsch. With regard to the latter, Krauss comments, "To fill out the expanded field, there is kitsch as the combination of memory and its opposite (non-memory). In this position, kitsch operates the way mass-produced substances (Formica) fake the artisanal originals (wood carving) that they can only remember through the lightest of counterfeits." In contrast to kitsch: "The combination of forgetting and not forgetting would be the *technical support*, where the need to forget exhausted mediums (like oil painting) nonetheless recalls *moments* in their histories."[14] This claim, it seems to me, is one way of indicating the instantiation of a contemporary ethos.

5th Procedure: Assemblage Work

Krauss approves and cites Stanley Cavell's formulation of the general problem: "The problem now posed by modernism is no longer to produce another instance of an art but a new medium within it."[15] One can assert something similar for anthropology today. The problem is not to produce another case, however updated with theory and the day's discursive politics. Rather, the challenge for some of us at least is to experiment with a new medium within the human sciences.

How to do it? A diagram of the problem-space is too grand, but elements for such a topological diagram can be assembled piecemeal. At this juncture, contrasts prove helpful.

A *theory* seeks examples in order to demonstrate its larger and more comprehensive claims. The demonstration ultimately is not a proof, strictly speaking, but it is a kind of prearranged test (*épreuve*). It might lead to some minor tweaking of elements or aspects of the theory, or, more often, it can be used to pick out or emphasize details in an example whose significance might otherwise be overlooked.

A *hypothesis* also calls for examples to be tested against. Modifications are more likely under these conditions, and less is at stake. Hypothesis testing is extremely rare in the human sciences. It has become less and less available for public scrutiny in the biosciences. Admitting experiments whose results did not confirm the initial hypothesis (and the grant proposal that buttressed it) is not admired or much discussed today.

Inquiry works on situations of breakdown and/or insufficient clarity. Dewey claims that the result of a process of inquiry is resolution and the establishment of a totality or whole. Regardless (and that last claim needs to be considered at more length), a successful inquiry should lead to further inquiry. A problem resolved might well make visible related problems that could not be posed with any rigor or even recognized without the preceding inquiry and its results. In the best of cases, problems ramify.

Assemblage work is related to inquiry but not identical with it. For me it has been driven by an unfocused but insistent curiosity. I have been drawn to the work of Gerhard Richter and the situations that he has contributed to surrounding himself with. The reasons for this nagging and insistent curiosity are not self-evident; attempting to clarify them is a primary motivation for undertaking the work. That being said, such clarification is not aimed at developing, improving, or refuting a theory or worldview as it is in the case of Krauss. Nor is it the work of hypothesis testing; if anything the practice seems to work the other way around. Living with, grappling with, and returning to aspects of Richter's work opens for me the need to find or to develop concepts and an ethos that helps formulate clearer ideas—and to reduce the nagging sense of not having a complete or adequate understanding of what he has been doing even while being in awe of it.

Assemblage work and, in a different mode, the things and objects with which it operates is riven, saturated, and at times clarified by the second-order observation and participation of the anthropologist. This work is not traditional criticism, either artistic or scientific. It is not judgmental except in the larger sense that John Dewey made of it: clarification of correct terminology. No one in the art world doubts that Richter's work is significant in the sense of innovative, enriching, and the usual range of hand-waving modifiers. Is its singularity what makes Richter's work significant? Or are these the wrong questions?

What is significant about it for an anthropologist? Not in the sense of how it can be used in a theoretical manner. Adjacency obstinately refuses such translation work or instrumental trading. So what does it do? Perhaps the work of assemblage work is to produce some pleasure in the articulation of not only figures of truth but also of the good and, above all, of forms of experience that provide openings and illuminations burrowed within a blood-soaked, market-dominated, bureaucratically expansive, and generally dreary moment in our time.

Object: On Not Keeping One's Distance: Uncle Rudi

Distance is not a safety-zone but a field of tension. It is manifested not in relaxing the claim of ideas to truth, but in delicacy and fragility of thinking.
—Theodor Adorno

Art historian John J. Curley provides a beautiful demonstration of what one might call "denunciation's blinders" (my term, not his).[16] Gerhard Richter has been the subject of criticism for depicting what appear to be representational portrayals of Nazi scenes ranging from German bombers to the figure in the best-known painting of this subgenre, *Uncle Rudi*. Curley writes, "Gerhard Richter's 1965 photo-painting *Onkel Rudi* (Uncle Rudi) depicts the painter's Nazi uncle in his Wehrmacht uniform. All interpretations of the painting emphasize this point."[17] Curley continues:

> Could it be, however, with its specific title and German military iconography, that Richter has overdetermined the meaning of this canvas — thereby willfully repressing other possible interpretations? Following this logic, I would like to begin with another question: How could Richter, in 1965, paint a soldier in front of *a* wall without evoking *the* Wall?[18]

Curley demonstrates with great force and clarity that Richter almost certainly could not paint a solider in front of a wall in 1965 without evoking the Berlin Wall.

Here is the narrative evidence (these facts are taken directly from Curley's article). East German authorities began building the wall on 13 August 1961. Gerhard Richter and his wife had crossed over to West Berlin to stay a few months earlier. Richter had a show in Berlin at the René Block Gallery in 1965. He participated in the September 1965 *Hommage à Berlin* show, which took the divided city as its theme. Richter exhibited *Onkel Rudi* twice in Berlin: at a solo exhibition at René Block in 1966 and a second time at the same gallery in a political show, *Hommage à Lidice*. "Two of the first three showings of the painting were in Berlin, a city full of uniformed guards, and defined by an extremely prominent wall." [19] It was also shown in Prague as part of the same show. It was closed down when Soviet tanks rolled into the city. Richter donated it to the Czech government after the end of the Cold War.

The uniforms of the East German National People's Army resembled those of the Wehrmacht. Rudi's hat and coat are similar to what East German soldiers wore. The wall's patterning appeared to be similar to the façades of East German administrative buildings. Richter's signature blur at that stage of his career further heightened the ambiguity.

How this and other paintings or, as Richter would insist later on, these images (*Bilder*) could be assigned a simple meaning is puzzling. As is well known, and has been discussed poignantly and pertinently by W. G. Sebald, Alexander Kluge, and others, any depiction of Germans who were not overtly victims or resisters during the war was charged with such an intense affect so as to be more or less impossible or at least perilous to exhibit.

During the same period, Richter had also produced an image of his niece who had been disabled, confined to an asylum, and killed by the Nazis. Two figures, barely visible in the background, with their backs turned to the viewer, may well be, it is plausible to claim, Nazi officials or even the executioners. This painting has been taken as a counterpoint or compensatory image to Uncle Rudi. It has received less critical commentary, as portraying victims is acceptable. One question remains in this register: was Uncle Rudi a victim?

On Keeping One's Distance: *Faits Divers*

Or are both of these paintings/images better understood as instances within the genre of *faits divers*? Here we rejoin the work of Alexander Kluge and reenter a zone that is beyond moralism even if it retains or provokes an uncanny critical affect.

What is the affect produced if we are not dealing directly with a representational realm of the artist's intentions? The courage to introduce complexity, ambiguity, and blurred lines in 1965 by a German artist needs to be underlined. It needs to be affirmed as well, even a half-century later because a great cloud or fog of political correctness covers the cultural critical discursive realm today.

Perhaps at issue is not Kluge's *faits divers* that turns on anonymity and the elusive fact/fiction distinction. With Uncle Rudi we have, at first glance at least, the opposite of anonymity; we have a specific and particular naming. Furthermore, we are not in doubt, at first glance at least, as to whether the subject is fact or fiction. Uncle Rudi was Gerhard Richter's uncle. Uncle Rudi was a Nazi soldier.

That Uncle Rudi could be named, pictured, and discussed by Richter in interviews and documented by righteous art critics, who could then indulge in serious discussions about the meaning of the representation, is itself a fact. But, as usual, facts are not the whole story; moreover, Gerhard Richter is not a historian or an art critic but an artist.

Here Curley's carefully thought-through intervention disrupts the comfortable positionality of prior critics. It reveals that, at the very least, their distance from their object of analysis was badly gauged. Adorno provides a formulation that seems to explain at least one dynamic of this (at least partial) misinterpretation.

> But as soon as thought repudiates its inviolable distance and tries with a thousand subtle arguments to prove its literal correctness, it founders. If it leaves behind the medium of virtuality, of anticipation that cannot be wholly fulfilled by any single piece of actuality; in short, if instead of interpretation, it seeks to become mere statement, everything it states becomes, in fact, untrue.[20]

Once criticism becomes "mere statement," which it then seeks to reflect on and provide commentary about, it "becomes, in fact, untrue." If what Richter was doing was providing a first-order representation, then the facts of the case would have been simply encompassed by a statement. But Richter has never provided first-order representations per se of anything. He is an artist, not an illustrator.

Richter, it turns out, was experimenting with ways of keeping his distance from representations. Many of his critics were not. They failed to see what was before them. Their insistence on the political and moral facts of the case blinded them. Adorno once again is helpful:

> Cowed into wanting to be no more than a mere provisional abbreviation for the factual matter beneath it, thought loses not only its autonomy in the face of reality, but with it the power to penetrate reality. Only at a remove from life can the mental life exist, and truly engage the empirical.[21]

The critics had cowed themselves, heads held high, with copies of their judgments in hand, carefully copyedited no doubt.

In 1965, Richter, it does not seem farfetched to claim, was seeking to establish an adjacency to the historical present. By portraying Uncle Rudi in his Wehrmacht uniform, he created a distance from the GDR border guards, all too present for all to see at the time. This distance, this adjacency, at least, was one means of truly engaging "the empirical." Of course, the empirical was not a thing. It was not even an object. Engaging it required a much more interesting and subtle relation to the present.

Another of Adorno's trenchant maxims gives us pause and provides some aid:

> The distance of thought from reality is itself nothing other than the precipitate of history in concepts. To use them without distance is, despite all the resignation it implies or perhaps because of it, a child's affair. For thought must aim beyond its target just because it never quite reaches it, and positivism is uncritical in its confidence of doing so, imagining its tergiversations to be due to mere conscientiousness.[22]

What, however, if Richter was dealing not with concepts but with images *Bilder*?

At the time, Richter was deploying one mode of distancing, from representations, from the present. It was a challenge to which he frequently returned, early on and for decades to come. He was experimenting with means of unsettling the viewer's distance and hence what the viewer was seeing. Richter was first recognized for his use of the blur. This technique has been discussed previously. The technique was a second-order one; Richter was seeking a form to engage, to use Niklas Luhmann's ponderous formulation, observers observing observers. Perhaps here it would be better to say: viewers viewing viewers.

Later on, Richter developed a technique of brushstrokes that appeared one way from afar and another close up. With *Onkel Rudi*, the medium was working on a different technological support—the photograph and the blur.

Strikingly, the politically correct and morally righteous failed to recognize that their own medium was not Richter's. It was only after Richter had achieved great fame that the archives of the former GDR became available, that a different and better historical distance could be, and was, articulated. Thus, a more rigorous adjacency came into being, one that allowed for more political complexity, sharper ethical observations, and more engaged, and truer, interpretations. Only then could we see what was there to see.

What it means is not the artist's domain. Now that time has passed, that the technological support of historical detail has become available and has been put to good use, the question of the medium for criticism becomes possible.

Adjacency: Moving Ratios

Mark Godfrey, one of the chief curators of the major retrospective of Richter's work entitled *Gerhard Richter: Panorama* (Tate Modern, London; Centre Pompidou, Musée national d'art moderne, Paris; Neue Nationalgalerie, Berlin), contributed an intriguing chapter, "Damaged Landscapes," to the exhibition's catalogue.[23] There are several fascinating sections in the piece, but the one that directly concerns our themes deals with a series of roughly fifty paintings Richter made during the late 1960s that Godfrey provocatively entitles "The Townscapes."

These are two types of townscapes that appear quite distinct at first but develop a ramifying relationship in Godfrey's essay. The first type is drawn from a series of photographs of architectural models "rendered with broad strokes in a range of grey tones." Richter affirmed the "dystopian feeling of these paintings, which represent post-war architecture as sterile or inhospitable."[24] They echo the reigning reaction against the stripped-down high modernism currently being built. Richter himself had architectural ambitions, although his projects were never built, and consequently paid close attention in a professional sense to the housing and public buildings being built.

The second type of townscape was drawn from aerial photographs. Richter selected a series of photographs from his collections in the *Atlas* and used a technique he had been experimenting with for some time: projecting the images onto a blank canvas. He had developed a style in which the photograph was used as a baseline image, often of the everyday, which he rendered realistically through careful application of paint, only to be disrupted by blurring and brushstrokes of wet paint as a finishing touch.

With these townscapes Richter shifted technique: instead of precise, fine brushwork he moved to thick brushstrokes and quickly applied dabs of paint. The results were striking and original, producing what Godfrey convincingly calls "a remarkable viewing experience." Seen from the normal distance one might adopt when entering a gallery (five meters), the canvases appeared to represent cities or, more precisely, townscapes. As the viewer approaches a canvas, however, things change:

> The image, no longer recognizable as an aerial view, disintegrates into its constituent dabs, smears and strokes of grey, dirty whites and blacks. [. . .] Your attention is absorbed by the haphazard array of brushwork and by the conundrum of how Richter knew that such brushwork would read, from farther away, as part of an identifiable image.[25]

Richter had succeeded in inventing a technique that reversed the usual experience of viewing paintings. Usually, the closer one gets, the details get clearer—but not in these paintings. One can say that at the time, whatever else was going on, Richter was experimenting with working over a standard technological support and turning it into a medium whose parameters, capacities, and affordances remained to be discovered: "The Townscapes become even more interesting when we think about their fracture and the viewing experience described above. The image disintegrates in the course of the viewer's approach and the painting transforms into a gestural abstract canvas."[26] Perhaps one might say that Richter took what Michael Fried has turned into a commonplace of art criticism—the twinning of either absorption or theatricality as a viewing experience—and undermined both.

Materiality, Not Perspective

Richter's image work traversed the discourses of the war circulating in Germany in the 1960s, but he took them up in his own manner:

Close up, the Townscapes never have the look of bricks and rubble, but they do insist on materiality. We now appreciate another reversal: while an aerial photograph of a city is an image in which the materiality of that city is kept at a distance, Richter uses an aerial image to generate a material object to remind the viewer of the material aftermath of the bombings.[27]

It is important to underscore that Richter was not a theorist or a politician; he was experimenting with taking current technological supports and attempting to use them as a medium in which images could render things visible that the reigning historical image-making and discourse-making either obscured entirely or left ambiguous.

Although these reworked images were first shown in 1968, Richter only began commenting on them in 1986. A remark from Godfrey concerning what we can discern about Richter's practices is pertinent not only in this instance: "Richter never claimed to have *intended* to create a group of paintings reflecting on the aerial bombing of cities, but was rather *reminded* of this history only after looking at the pictures long after he made them."[28] Perhaps one could say that Richter, like everyone else, was to a significant degree situated in the multifarious determinations of his historical situation. Unlike most of his compatriots, however, Richter sought to establish an untimely and *intempestif* relation to his situation through image-making and what it could afford those willing to pay attention.

Futures Past

A radio lecture that Adorno gave in 1960, "The Meaning of Working through the Past," offers a frame to the challenge of portraying the destruction of German cities or anonymous cities. He cautioned against using the horrific destruction of Dresden and other German cities by the Allies as an equation, or even a balancing act, to Auschwitz. Adorno argued that both should be remembered in their historical settings and taken as cautions for future destructions to come.

Technē 3: Mirrors and Images: A Treacherous Simplicity

JT-P: Over the years, glass has become increasingly important in your work. In 1967 you made your first glass object, the "4 Panes of Glass." What is the essence of your relationship to glass? You noted on a sketch: "Glass—Symbol (see everything, understand nothing)." The closest things to the readymades are your mirrors. [. . .] What do you see in the mirror?

GR: Myself. But then I immediately see that it functions like a painting: just more perfectly. And just like a painting, it shows something that isn't there—at least not there where we see it.

JT-P: So the mirror would be the perfect artist?

GR: Exactly.

—Interview with Jan Thorn-Prikker, 2004

Gerhard Richter's first experiments with glass structures took place in 1965 ("4 Panes of Glass").[29] How to interpret his periodic return to these technological supports and the way he has used them is a troubling, if fascinating, question. For example, Benjamin Buchloh's chapter "Gerhard Richter's Eight Gray: Between *Vorschein* and *Glanz*" (*Vorschein* = anticipatory appearance; *Glanz* = gleam and glimmer) is the only interpretive essay in a book, formerly the catalogue, concerning a 2002 exhibition in Berlin of Richter's glass panels. The most prestigious and authoritative institutions of the German art world sponsored the exhibition and the book. One can assume that Richter allowed his friend Buchloh's essay to be included and thus featured as the interpretive frame for the exhibit and the work it contained. This practice of framing his artwork with high-theory essays and then distancing himself from them in his own interviews is one Richter has made in different ways consistently over the years, as we have seen.

The reason to include Buchloh's high-theory prose here is that I believe that what he had to say was characteristic of one style of art criticism at the time (elite university–based, high-theory, historical if not genealogical). I believe that it is part (with variants) of the assemblage within which Richter is restively allowing and curating his work to be situated. I believe that in its actuality Richter's work is utterly recalcitrant to Buchloh's style of discourse as well as its substantive claims. That very heterogeneity, however, seems to provide an essential condition for it to be brought into an assemblage with Richter's work by the artist himself with help from his entourage.

Of more interest to me is thinking about what Richter is doing— intentionally or not—by including Buchloh's essay. My answer is that Richter should be seen to be establishing an assemblage cast in a contemporary mode. If Richter were an avant-gardist seeking to overthrow the modernist tradition entirely, he would be a modern. Rather, he lets Buchloh make the modernist case in detail. Richter no doubt watches it self-destruct (as we shall see below); nonetheless, he respects his friend's views and style in their difference. It would seem that Buchloh assists Richter in his understanding of the history and current environment in which he works and therefore, indirectly at least, his artistic practice. To understand, naturally, is not to agree.

It follows that as what I am engaged in is anthropology and not art criticism, my observation of observers observing observers, to use Niklas Luhmann's phrase, differs from the perspective of those engaged more directly with the art world and with art criticism. Hence my approach is diagnostic of a configuration of the actual. For these and related reasons, I will quote Buchloh's prose at some length.

The contemporary, I claim, is a moving ratio in which the modern becomes historical. The contemporary, I claim, entails a relationship of adjacency. An anthropological ethos of the contemporary seeks to take into account active assemblage work through various forms of second-order observation and form-giving—with the aim thereby to invent a practice of anthropological assemblage work.

Modernist History: Buchloh's Narrative

Buchloh identifies what he calls "four paradoxes" or oppositions in Richter's work or, more accurately, his attempt to make sense of Richter's work:

1. The first opposition is the *public* dimension of the glass panels and the paradoxical *privacy* of contemplative experience that this painterly structure solicits.[30] How, Buchloh wonders, does Richter maintain a tension—if that is what he is doing—between these two poles?
2. The second opposition is between *seriality* and *monumentality*.[31] The serial is linked to commodity production and works against the auratic and the hieratic. How Buchloh wonders, does Richter maintain a tension—if that is what he is doing—between these two poles?
3. The third opposition is between Richter's record of *loss* and its seeming lack of *affect*. Buchloh quotes the photographer Jeff Wall as having posed the problem in general terms:

The gray volumes of conceptualism are filled with somber ciphers which express primarily the inexpressibility of socially critical thought in the form of art. They embody a terrible contradiction. These artists attempted to break out of the prison house of the art business, its bureaucracy and architecture, and to turn toward social life. But in that process they re-assumed the very emptiness they wished to put behind them.[32]

How Buchloh wonders, does Richter maintain a tension—if that is what he is doing—between modern art and social criticism?

4. The fourth opposition is the improbable synthesis of *void* and *transcendence*.[33] How, Buchloh wonders, does Richter maintain a tension—if that is what he is doing—between these two poles?

Buchloh proceeds through the major part of his essay to situate Richter's glass panels as if they were addressing this series of paradoxes as a set of phases in the narrative of the history of modernist painting in the twentieth century. Although his narrative reads to an outsider as if it were cast in a mode of pathos, it is probably better to see it as in the comedic mode. By this I mean that there are periodic, yet temporary, resolutions. These resolutions never endure, but neither do they discourage the actors sufficiently to cease in their efforts to manage things in order to arrive at a happier ending. The third alternative would be the tragic. The constant refrain within the modernist art world of the "end of painting" has been experienced as tragic. Recounting the "end of painting" as a series without end, however, tends toward the ironic, whether heroic or simply plodding.

Modernism: The Monochrome and the Window

Buchloh frames Richter's project as continuous with but also as a possible innovation in the core problem of modernist art: "to void the conventions of all pictorial representation and of all privileged forms of experience."[34] Buchloh rehearses the lineage of the modernist pictorial dialectic of purity and elimination, starting with the breakthrough moment of Malevich's *Black Square* (dated 1913) and Rodchenko's follow-up painting from 1921, *Red, Yellow, Blue*. Both were attempts to free painting from "the episteme of the window":

This duplicity (or historical ambiguity) that hesitates to abolish the memory of the painterly episteme within the very act of its radical deconstruction (an episteme that had, after all, determined painting's functions for centuries) would become the starting point for a series of key Modernist works that have engaged painting's containment within that episteme, from Delaunay's *Windows*, to Marcel Duchamp's *Fresh Window* (1920), from Josef Albers's glass assemblages such as his *Park* (1924) made from industrial glass to Ellsworth Kelly's *Window* for the Kabinett für aktuelle Kunst in Bremerhaven in 1970–71. It is within this lineage, as much as within the history of monochrome painting, that Richter's *Eight Gray* and his earlier works of glass must be situated.[35]

Or:

Richter's *Eight Gray* shares these premises of a critique of occularcentrism. It is a work in which the institutional restriction of art and its ensuing condemnation to a tautology have been formulated with a clarity that programmatically *deprivileges* vision rather than celebrating it.[36]

Or:

Thus Richter's monochromes and glass and mirror works are not only erasures, probing the purity of negation and the sobriety of withdrawal. Richter's *Eight Gray* also asks what kind of spectatorial subject would be inscribed within this architecture of effacement and elimination. Could *Eight Gray* generate the same type of spatiality that determined the monochrome voids of the architecture in Strand's photograph [*Wall Street, New York*], a tectonics of oppression, melancholia, and silence? Or would it generate the opposite, a space of mirror inscriptions where the new subject would suture itself in the architectural dimension of reflective glass, but a painterly construction that would at the same time preserve the memory of its Modernist self-reflexivity and empirical skepticism?[37]

There are echoes of Foucault's use of the concept of the *episteme*. Added to it are deconstructive and structuralist terms such as "spectatorial subject," "inscribed," and "suture." These terms are set within larger parametric terms such as "architecture," "generate," "determine," "techtonics," and "dimensions."

Ultimately, for Buchloh, there is inevitability and coherence to Richter's use of the mirror. Thus:

Richter's mirror paintings suggest that the monochrome surface, in its total eradication of the indexical inscription of any mark-making process, inevitably *has* to become a mirror, or a spatial and architectural membrane in which spectatorial movement inscribes itself as the sole source of perceptual activity. Thus it establishes a dialectic between aesthetic device and spectatorial participation that can adequately reflect the necessary conditions of radical equality and equivalence between aesthetic experience of the spectator and aesthetic conception of the artist.[38]

This highly constructivist, analytic, and voluntaristic summation proceeds from the way Buchloh has posed the problem. It is a discursive solution, but one can doubt that it captures Richter's artistic practice and productions.

Variables, Not Concepts: The Glass Problem

JS: Were you influenced by Duchamp?

GR: I knew Duchamp's work and certainly there was an influence. It may have been an unconscious antagonism—because his painting *Nude Descending a Staircase* rather irritated me. I thought very highly of it but I could never accept that it had put paid to a certain kind of painting. So I did the opposite and painted a "conventional" nude. But, as I said, it was an unconscious process not a strategy. The same happened with *4 Panes of Glass*. Something of Duchamp did not suit me—all the mystery mongering—and that is why I painted these simple glass panes and showed the whole windowpane problem in a completely different light.

—Interview with Jonas Storsve, 1991

Or:

GR: What attracted me about my mirrors was the idea of having nothing manipulated in them. A piece of bought mirror; just hung there, without any addition, to operate immediate and directly. Even at the risk of being boring. Mere demonstration. The mirrors, and even more the *Panes of Glass*, were also certainly directed against Duchamp, against his *Large Glass*.

—Interview with Hans Ulrich Obrist, 1993

Buchloh is honest, sincere, and even heroic in his search for a framework to interpret Richter's work. His quest for a *Magister Ludi*-type of solution, like that of the master gamesman in Hesse's novel, despite its virtuosity, none-theless ultimately proves unsatisfactory to its practitioner.

> It becomes apparent then that some of the difficulties posed by Richter's *Eight Gray* result from the fact that the large-scale gray glass panes can neither be fully mapped onto the historical formation of the monochrome nor can they be exclusively seen through the episteme of painting as win-dow.[39]

He means the difficulties for a certain style of art criticism.

He continues to wonder about his own dilemma: "Thus, in a way *Eight Gray* is an installation whose range of historical references—and references of considerable magnitude, as we have attempted to sketch out—is sur-passed by its temporal and spatial specificity."[40] "Surpassed" is a residual term from the repertoire of a once dominant dialectic manner of interpret-ing situations. There are other frames, however, that would not have been doubled over into these paroxysms of paradox in the first place.

Admirably, Buchloh concludes by taking a step away from his determin-istic meta-narratives and a step closer to criticism of Richter's work in quite different terms.

> What Richter's stainless paintings reflect first of all then are these ques-tions: When does erasure achieve perfection and when does it end up merely as polish? When would the perfection of erasure signal a sealed repression and when would the shiny surface merely entrap the gaze in a fetishistic exchange?[41]

We call this shift in register a move from concepts to variables. It seems, how-ever, that the concepts Buchloh draws from one line of art criticism have not proved to be appropriate to the discordances and indeterminations he feels and sees. Hence he ends with open-ended questions that border on the rhe-torical or the desperate. An alternative diagnosis: the problem lies not with Richter's artwork but with Buchloh's discourse. Richter writes:

> Any thoughts on my part about the "construction" of a picture are false, and if the execution works, this is only because I partly destroy it, or be-cause it works in spite of everything—by not detracting and not looking the way I planned.

I often find this intolerable, and even impossible to accept, because, as a thinking, planning human being, it humiliates me to find out that I am so powerless. It casts doubt on my competence and my constructive ability. My only consolation is to tell myself that I did actually make the pictures—even though they are a law unto themselves, even though they treat me any way they like and somehow just take shape. Because it is still up to me to determine the point at which they are finished (picture-making consists of a multitude of yes/no decisions, with a Yes to end it all). If I look at it that way, the whole thing starts to seem quite natural again—or rather Nature-like, alive—and the same thing applies to the comparison on the social level.[42]

CONTEMPORARY CONSOLATIONS   Unconsoled

> Ultimately it is a question of showing the departures from
> meaning (*sens*), not the arrivals.
> **—Bernard Comment on Roland Barthes**

Gerhard Richter has made us a gift of his extravagantly flourishing work in its many varieties over the course of the decades. The ever-expanding secondary literature has not converged on a unified understanding or even a common approach to his work. In my view, this lack of an agreed-upon synthesis is both appropriate and gratifying. Richter has shown himself to be durably restive in his activity and steadfastly recalcitrant in his responses to those attempting to impose an essence on his activity. That being said, it is also the case that Richter invites, contributes to, and in some cases encourages much of this expansive and heterogeneous outpouring of commentary. Naturally, I am aware of the fact that I too am participating in this meandering, interpretive pageant.

Form

Roland Barthes's second course (1978) after his appointment at the Collège de France preceding his death in March 1980 (from injuries after being struck by a truck on his way home from the Collège) was entitled "*Le Neutre*," "The Neutral."[1]

Professors at the Collège de France had few demands placed on them. Aside from lecturing each year on their "research," they were required to submit a summary of the last year's teaching as well as conduct a seminar. In part, here is the way Barthes characterized his theme:

We have defined as pertaining to the Neutral every inflection that, dodging or baffling the paradigmatic, oppositional structure of meanings, aims at the suspension of the conflictual basis of discourse.

By means of successive strokes, various references, and free digressions, we have tried to make it understood that the Neutral does not necessarily correspond to the flat, utterly depreciated image that the doxa assumes but could constitute a strong active value.[2]

This ambitious, pathos-laden (in the sense that it knows that it is fated to fall short of its desired goals), and self-implosive program has as its ultimate goal the invention and practice of a distinctive ethos of thought and life.

Barthes's commenting on his own pedagogy and style of thinking, here as elsewhere, underscores a rhythm and mode of composition that intentionally returns repeatedly upon itself, multiplies digressions, and purposively violates expectations of a linear narrative or traditionally logical development, both of which he is seeking to undermine. His early work *Le degré zéro de l'écriture* (*Writing Degree Zero*), set the problem of language to which he returned throughout his life, time after time, in different manners and with different forms.[3]

A distinctive characteristic of Barthes's writing as well as his thought was the prominence he gave to fragments and citations. Why?

In my personal thematic, the fragment does not oppose itself paradigmatically to the totality, but rather to "*la nappe*," to content, to that which flows in an uninterrupted fashion, infinite, and whose caricatural forms, the farce-forms, are found in the knowledge world, the dissertation for example.[4]

One must add the obligation of unlinking [*déliaison*] is not the simple fact of a disgust or fatigue; it is politically founded.[5]

Unveiling is not just taking off the veil but dismembering it [*dépiécer*].[6]

The scope of claims here is expansive, ranging from the political to knowledge practices, to those of narrative, and ultimately, to those of ethics. All of the "undoing words"—*déliaison*, *dévoiler*, and *dépiécer*—are not casually or inadvertently used. For Barthes, they are the heart of the matter: they embody a highly self-conscious and stylized recalcitrance against a mode of expression and a way of life that he often named "bourgeois," although today that appellation seems dated while the problem does not.

Problem: A Form for the Neutral

In addition to the publication and translation of notes from Barthes's course, there is an excellent interpretive book on the importance of the place of *le Neutre* in all of Barthes's work. The book is by Bernard Comment and is entitled *Roland Barthes, vers le neutre*. Comment underscores the problematic or fundamentally self-contradictory framing of Barthes's project: Barthes's attempts to use language to derail language. Barthes's project is self-consciously self-annihilating. Or perhaps it is simply perilous to the point of dizziness: "how to think the '*hors-sens*' in language when language is precisely the framework of sense?"[7] How does Barthes proceed with this vertiginous project? One answer would be to imagine a form of utopia where utter transparency and immediacy would reign. Another would be to think not of a u-topia but of an a-topia. These are not the directions Barthes takes; rather, knowing full well the recklessness (or foolhardiness) of his project, he adopts a kind of *fuite en avance*. Comment names this Escher-like attempt to both identify and escape the rules of the game of meaning and knowledge as a *protension* (a drawing out, an extension). It is that toward which "one tends, that toward what one can only tend, as if toward a 'chimerical horizon.' Not through a simple transgression therefore (which could itself be a prisoner of the binary for/against), but an escape beyond meaning."[8] Barthes's self-awareness of the recklessness of the task is matched only by his sense of being caught, uncomfortably so, inevitably so, in the web of language and discourse, a web he described provocatively, if self-indulgently, in his inaugural lecture at the Collège de France as "fascist."[9]

Modes of *Pathosformel*

Such a search is self-consciously nonrealistic, if ultimately pragmatic, and acknowledged by Barthes as being so. It resolutely and recalcitrantly seeks a form adequate to its pathos, its striving and incompletion. In that light, we can appreciate two of Barthes's meta-claims: "The course exists because there is a desire for the Neutral: a pathos";[10] and "The desire for the Neutral continually stages a paradox: as an object, the Neutral means suspension of violence; as a desire it is violent."[11] Here I will take up only three modulations of the mood of the affect field of pathos—*ataraxia*, arrogance, and *kairos.* They can be arrayed as a series so as to show the deficient, excessive, and virtue range of how Barthes treats pathos as affect.

Barthes is hyper-aware that his efforts were (and indeed had to be) pathos-riven. Not only was he driven to pursue the Neutral for his own reasons of temperament; he was also conscious of assigning himself maximally only an ephemeral success. The mood of the Neutral and the affect field within which it operates, or has operated within at different times (whose *Nachleben* Barthes is ever attentive to identifying and drawing lessons from) and to which it contributes, proves to be an unstable and elusive topic for Barthes. He is not seeking—quite to the contrary—to develop a theory of *pathos* or even to fix a concept; rather, he is identifying a narrative topic that will provide equipment in the older sense of the term for thinking and practice.

In addition to the central rhetorical register of passion, there is a second sense of pathos: the theatrical. Barthes's courses were carefully staged, and he dwelled on how others staged their texts and gestures. He was equally the director of these productions; what was achieved (or failed to be achieved) was designed to affect the audience as well as the director himself.

A third register of pathos is the medical, or more precisely, the pathological. Throughout this course (and Bernard Comment shows how this thematic was a long-lasting one in Barthes's work and life) Barthes makes repeated use of quotations from Japanese and Chinese sources and traditions; the West was, had been, and was almost certainly going to continue to be pathological in the strict sense of "ill" from its (pathos)logos: "A thought of pathos (the active-affective) should not be looked for in a meta-discourse (-logies) but in . . . the power of being affected [which] does not necessarily mean passivity but affectivity, sensibility, sentiment."[12] A substantial portion of the course was devoted to the search for instances and forms of affectivity, sensibility, and sentiment that can render possible the Neutral as well as those that reduce or wither it. What solace, if any, the specification of these topics provides remains unanswered and underspecified.

Barthes attends to both the Stoic philosophers and the Sophists. Ultimately he wants to find or create a way of acting that is adjacent to both of them with their core ethical concepts of *ataraxia* and *apathy*.[13] The exemplar of the quest for the Neutral is the philosopher Pyrrho. Fortunately for Barthes, there are no surviving texts from Pyrrho, although there are many stories that circulated later about his life and practices. There is no current agreement among the specialists about which of the contradictory positions attributed to him are the worthiest of credence.[14] Barthes is, of course, aware of this absence of consensus or evidence; he coyly draws a sharp distinction between Pyrrho and the later school whose name—Pyrrhonism—is attached to the (non)founder.

Pyrrho was weary of the philosophic debates of his time. An anecdote Barthes repeats a number of times concerns a disciple of Pyrrho, Eurylochus; he jumped into a nearby river to get away from his students, who were pressing him with questions that he found pointless and irritating.[15] He was weary of the game but his weariness yielded action: "Weariness is thus creative, from the moment, perhaps, when one agrees to submit to its orders. New things are thus born out of lassitude—from being fed up."[16] It is the cultivation and practice of this type of pragmatic refusal to accept the given that instantiates the imperative for the Neutral if not its form.

Excess and Deficiency: Arrogance, Anorexia

There are attitudes, practices, values, and norms that encourage debilitating states. Barthes groups them and distributes them in several ways during his course.[17]

One of the central groupings—of beliefs, concepts, values, attitudes, and practices that Barthes implicitly qualifies as *excess* of the pathos of the Neutral—he names as arrogance. Barthes links the games of knowledge and those of ethics in regard to their mutual enhancements and disruptions. The foundational move of arrogance is to make a demand in a specific form that forecloses what might count as a response other than in the terms offered. He identifies this refusal of the recognition of others as an ethical shortcoming and a blind spot; it is the anchor point of arrogance.

> I gather all the linguistic "gestures" that work as discourses of intimidation, of subjection, of domination, of assertion, of haughtiness: that claim the authority, the guarantee of a dogmatic truth or of a demand that does not think, that does not conceive of the other's desire.[18]

The "pure" form of arrogance is the demand for interpretation. Its essential strategy is the claim to put forth "evidence" as unchallengeable; its goal is to shut down discussion, exchange, and motion. The pure act of arrogance is to declare as evident "that which one wishes to see prevail." Such strategic attempts of closure are common in knowledge games but also in ethical, political, and amorous ones as well. This gambit of setting the rules of the game—and a form of power that attempts to enforce compliance—is the elementary form of arrogance.

Barthes's unexpected type case of *deficiency* in the pathos of the Neutral is "anorexia": the acceptance or retreat into a state of compliance to the arrogant demands not to eat, speak, or think. The response is, to a degree, active, but it is destructive, even pathological, and in no way opens the way for escape from such commands or reproaches.

Virtue: *Kairos*

Barthes takes up the term *kairos* and arrays a number of the concepts that have been embedded in it historically and, adding his own, links it with the Neutral: "The etymology for *Ho Kairos*: a fitting measure, just, a fitting moment, opportune. Occasion—'it is time, it is the moment.'"[19] The challenge is to identify and meet the need for the Neutral to be specific and relate to the particularity of an occasion—its contingence, its conjuncture, its "à propos."

Barthes cites with approval a fragment (#159) from Blaise Pascal's *Pensées I*: "We must know where to doubt, where to feel certain, where to submit."[20] It is Pascal's use of "where" that, for Barthes, focuses attention on this type of *kairos*.

Protagoras, Barthes tells us, proclaimed that he had developed and could put into practice a total science; consequently, he could always find the right way of intervening rhetorically in any situation and apropos of any topic.[21] To the degree that the Skeptic philosophers maintained a consistent position regardless of the situation or the topic under consideration, they ran the risk of turning themselves against their principles of skepticism with a dogmatic position holders who always knew how to intervene and hence always knew what was at stake.

Richter: Restive & Recalcitrant

At least at times, often during periods of stasis, the drive for the Neutral could be said to characterize Gerhard Richter's practice and ethos. His interviews are rife, if one listens, with sensitivity to the pitfalls of arrogance, the attunement to *kairos*, and the overriding affect-fields of pathos.

There are, however, two obvious dimensions that separate Barthes and Richter. The first is that the bourgeoisie and its form of life do not haunt

Richter. Richter is not from a bourgeois background and was trained in a quite different tradition of the arts in the GDR. Rather, Richter is haunted by the totalitarian regimes of the twentieth century and to a lesser extent by consumer capitalism, which he has found ways of accommodating, having developed a certain reserve, a certain adjacency, and a great deal of success. Perhaps one could say he has self-consciously, over time, negotiated (with himself and those around him) the price to be paid for access to the relative freedom to engage in his image-making.

The second difference is an obvious one: Richter is a painter, not a writer. Although he seeks to free his painting from the labyrinth of dead ends— which its history and recent past might seem to have enclosed it in—he does so, and successfully as far as I am concerned, through image-making. As he put it in an interview with Alexander Kluge, "Sometimes I think I shouldn't call myself a painter but rather a maker of images (*Bildermacher*). I am more interested in images than in painting."[22] Richter, I am claiming, has invented a contemporary mode of passage out of the double binds his co-practitioners struggle with over and over. His interviews articulate in different terms a commitment to affect degree zero (gray paintings, mirrors and glass) while he continues to produce effervescent work after work, albeit often with somber overtones and saturated with some of Europe's darkest *Nachleben*. We have seen him dodge and then develop strategies for assembling the arrogant (critics and others) while staying adjacent to them. We have seen his vigilant attention and discernment to various turning points, *kairoi*, macro and micro, as opportunities to experiment and create somewhat differently (images rather than representations or abstractions). Richter has not fled his interlocutors by swimming across a river in order to escape those seeking to understand what he is attempting to do.

Elements of a Contemporary Ethos: Unconsoled and Disappointed

Suddenly, I became completely indifferent to not being modern.
    And like a blind person whose finger gropes along life's text and recognizes here and there what had already been said.
—Roland Barthes

A French philosopher, Michaël Fœssel, published a book in 2015 entitled *Le temps de la consolation (The Time of Consolation)*.[23] It is intriguing, sweeping in historical scope, abstract to the outer limits as such French philosophical essays tend to be; in its reckless audacity, however, it does provide a challenging diagnostic of the situation of *anthrōpos* today. The book's core claim is that until Modernity—by which the author means the triumph of method as the road to knowledge, primarily associated with Descartes—philosophy was thought to provide a source and guide to a healing consolation for the ills with which humans were chronically afflicted. Finitude was answered by a range of sources of consolation grounded by philosophers in a comprehensive metaphysics or ontology and later by a register of the transcendental. For Fœssel, until modernity, the claims to consolation lay in the arts and realm of memory. As hard as the present might be to endure for an afflicted individual or community, there were times when things had been good, and the memory of those times was taken to be both reliable and consoling, thereby offering a balm to the present troubles. As Fœssel operates uniquely in the realm of ideas, anthropologists or others wondering how effective the solace provided (whether by Platonists, Stoics, or Christians) really had been in peoples' lives will not find any answers.

Fœssel from time to time draws on the late courses of Michel Foucault, especially *The Hermeneutics of the Subject: Lectures at the Collège de France, 1981–1982*, where Foucault outlines and defends in some detail the claim that (again) at least until the time of Descartes, philosophy was a way of life that thought about, sought to experiment with, and find ways to articulate the relationships of care of the self with knowledge of the self. Once knowledge became secured through method, its form as a way of life began to change dramatically. Here is an instance of values (objective, depersonalized knowledge) gradually coming to the fore. Not only care of the self but also an integration of the will to know, or to obtain truth, gradually gained a relative autonomy. The price to be paid for this drive for autonomy of objective knowledge to be available through method to whoever could apply the relevant procedures was, among other things, the separation of value spheres, at least in an incipient form.

As the shaping of a way of life of knowledge production revealed its immense power, the price to be paid for its achievements only slowly became apparent. This process and its affect is perhaps best captured in the Faust stories from the earlier versions still infused with magic through Goethe and ultimately Max Weber with his bleak and unflinching claim that modern knowledge (*Wissenschaft, all domains of rigorous, methodologically guided knowledge*) had achieved utter separation from the meaning of human life whether in the spheres of suffering, creation, or affect. Knowledge and consolation were divorced.

Consolation

In his last three years of courses, Foucault was attempting to think his way through, and perhaps out of, his diagnostic of the Faustian situation of modern philosophy. He was successful in providing a plausible diagnosis and a genealogy of the problem-space. He died too young to have provided a path beyond Faust.

Fœssel is far less rigorous and scholarly in his essayistic narrative than Foucault, but his diagnosis of late modernity does offer us some lines of thought to pursue. Let us follow Fœssel in drawing a few distinctions.

First, the arts and sciences of consolation had been and might become, once again reinvented on different principles and in a different setting with different goals, what Fœssel, following Foucault, calls "techniques of the self." Such techniques were designed to afford a suffering subject the possibility as well as the means of finding a path beyond Faust: "Consolation belongs to the 'techniques of the self,' which allow the suffering being to constitute himself as an active subject of his own existence."[24]

Second, given the backgrounding or loss of these older techniques of the self, the first step is to provide a diagnosis that renders visible the problem-space of what has been lost. This work entails an acknowledgment that the person in a state of distress must have some sense that a form of consolation had once been possible and remains desirable. "It is a question of elaborating the themes, the concepts, or the procedures that impose themselves in place of the ancient models of consolation."[25]

Third, there is no consolation without desolation, and it is only on the latter term that philosophy can contribute its insights. Fourth, under conditions of modernity (or late modernity) consolation becomes a critical tool once it is taken up as a desire and not as a result. The figure who embodies this ethos is "the unconsoled" whose sadness marks an ethical protest. Although Fœssel does not use this language, it is useful to organize ethical claims in terms of excess, deficiency, and the middle term or virtue.

Excess: Reconciliation

The *excess* term for Fœssel is "reconciliation." Although the term covers a wide range of instances, its claim is that sadness, melancholy, loss, and related states can be overcome whether through therapy or conformity to norms of an untroubled life. The first step in the direction of excess is to posit a positive identification of what has been lost and to reject any acceptance of such states of finitude. For Fœssel the core response in modernity to such feeling of loss and hope for consolation is the narrative: "Reconciliation abolishes suffering retrospectively: consolation replies to the suffering of suffering by giving it the means of narration."[26] There is a price to be paid for constructing such narratives of reconciliation and making them believable. That price amounts to bad faith: the narrative as a therapeutic or theological or philosophical instrument for achieving relief of suffering and motion toward reconciliation works to the degree that the very instrument that promises relief or resolution must be forgotten as a fiction, an artifice.

Deficit: Melancholy

The *deficit* term is melancholy or simply sadness. The subject tacitly accepts the state of lack of consolation for loss, whether personal or collective. Experience grows gray and static. We see this described both in modern narratives such as Goethe's *Faust* and in older ones. In the latter, presumably other actions were possible, whereas in the former the path ahead led toward reconciliation, a state of unrequited hopes.

The correlative term is nostalgia. Adorno, in his *Minima Moralia*, observes that "the idea according to which memories belong to us legitimately and accurately belongs to the arsenal of sentimental and impotent consolations."[27] Recognizing this state of affairs—both the sheer factuality of human finitude and suffering as well as the impossibility of finding consolation through memory—requires a certain fortitude, a certain heroic culture, if one is to measure up to the ethos of the situation. "The surest path toward desolation is the one that ignores the desolation that history has brought us."[28] There is no exit except acceptance of this finitude and the sudden realization that a different ethos might be invented and practiced.

Virtue: Unconsoled

The *virtue* term is to be and to wish to be unconsoled. Striving for this state entails being neither passive nor regressive. Rather it consists in imagining being consoled while remaining aware that whatever consolations are currently available will never be definitive as there is no ultimate restoration of a prior state of presumed well-being or wholeness.

For Fœssel, the figure of the unconsoled is that of modern man conscious of the irreparable ruptures and breaks of existence but still caring to respond through the invention of new ways of being together. In the recognition of this state of affairs, the irreconcilable perhaps constitutes the only way of having a future. It calls for an ethos of recalcitrance to the demands to adapt to the supposed facts of human existence's finitude.

By facing the present and facing toward the near future, Fœssel makes the striking diagnostic claim: "Our consolations have gained the right to be inventive."[29] He actually tells us little or nothing about the form such inventions might take—or have taken—and to that extent he remains a modern, albeit adopting an ethos of modern maturity.

Rather than either pointing to attempts to be inventive or proposing a form for such invention himself, Fœssel concludes: "Consolation for Moderns becomes hope."[30] Of the traditional sites of consolation—nature, language, and community—Fœssel holds out the most hope for political change, for new forms of community as well as a new language of politics, but offers neither cases nor narratives nor even sketches of what forms such coming together in a consolatory manner might take and how it might be discussed and narrated.

Language, Memory, and Nature

One aspect of Richter's elusiveness is that like others of his generation (Michel Foucault, Roland Barthes, Gilles Deleuze, and Alexander Kluge but not Pierre Bourdieu or Jürgen Habermas) he has dreamed of combining both an amiable antisubjectivity with an insistent nonrepresentational objectivity. Richter has sporadically sought to give form, to render some of its parameters visible, to this impossible couple within his experimental practice of artistic production. One of those proverbial parameters is nature.

Richter's views of nature are not easy to grasp although they are certainly meant to be against the grain of opinion, especially German opinion. Thus:

Of course, my landscapes are not only beautiful or nostalgic, with a Romantic or classical suggestion of lost Paradises, but above all "untruthful" [*verlogen* = mendacious] (even if I did not always find a way of showing it): and by "untruthful" I mean the glorifying way we look at nature — nature, which in all its forms is always against us, because it knows no meaning, no pity, no sympathy, because it knows nothing and is absolutely mindless; the total antithesis of ourselves, absolutely inhuman.[31]

But:

When I say I take form as my starting point, and that I would like content to evolve out of form (and not the reverse process, whereby a form is found to fit a literary idea), then this reflects my conviction that form, the cohesion of formal elements, the structure of the phenomenal appearance of matter (=form), generates a content, — and that I can manipulate the outward appearance as it comes, in such a way as to yield this or that content.

In this effort I am first of all supported by music (Schoenberg and all other pure music evolves out of its own laws, and not out of the effort to find a form for a specific statement); and, secondly, I find the essential confirmation in Nature, which produces material changes without any intention (or cause) related to content, but takes on this or that form in accordance with its own preconditions. The more complicated the process is, the more functional Nature's "contents," qualities, capabilities become. The issue of content is thus nonsense; i.e. there is nothing *but* form. There is only "something": there is only what there is.[32]

Perhaps we can say that nature for Richter might best be seen as a technological support; his quest is how to use it as a medium.

Steam and Mirrors

Richter's repeated return to the use of mirrors and of glass materials from quite early on in his career can be taken up as a privileged site of this impossible dream. Artist that he is, Richter has never simply installed a mirror in a gallery, or even a pane of glass, at least without calling attention to them as an echo of the tradition of the readymade. Richter's work, after all, recognizes and flourishes through his myriad manners of acknowledging *Nachleben*. When he finds a way—a form—of acknowledging them, he is on the way to a distinctive *Pathosformel*.

An art historian, Doris Krystof, contributed a short article entitled "Visual Speculations: Mirrors and Glass in the Work of Gerhard Richter" to the catalogue of an exhibit entitled *Gerhard Richter: Ohne Farbe = Without Color* at the Museum Franz Gertsch in Burgdorf, Switzerland, in 2005. I quote her remarks at some length because they seem to me to be a convincing (up to a point) and an intelligent summary of how Richter is approached by the professionals in the field as well as being indicative of the state of insights on his practice. She writes:

> Richter tackles the subject of glass and mirrors explicitly as a painter. He began in 1967 with the freestanding, movable installation titled *Vier Glasscheiben* (four panes of glass). Seen in conjunction with the artist's paintings of this period, it presents the idea of painting as a window as well as a means of conceptualizing the ever-changing perspectives and reference points in the perception of art. From this point on, the preoccupation with mirrors and glass runs through all of Richter's work. This interest has reached a new level with the glass-pane objects he has created since 2002—space-filling displays of semi-transparent panes set up parallel to one another, often braced within a metal framework. The panes, that appear to be misted by steam, offer a slightly confusing visual experience; they represent unfocussed and atmospheric elements, while their predecessors, the monochrome glass surfaces of the nineties, reflected the surrounding spaces with sharp-edged clarity. This is also particularly true of those commercially produced, clear crystal mirrors that Richter used in the eighties, ostentatiously giving them equal status to his paintings by numbering them as works of art and using the same pricing system for them as for the paintings. This conceptual gesture, based on Duchamp's Ready-mades, was an important statement of Richter's intention to create an understanding of painting stripped of any trace of subjective pathos.[33]

I think it is more accurate to say that Richter was *acknowledging* the legacy of Duchamp while not *basing* his work on Duchamp's. As we have seen, Richter fervently contests the view that he was imitating Duchamp or accepting his approach to art and publicity (*Ema* painting). Richter has expressed his irritation at the venerated manner with which the legacy of the readymade has been taken up in the art world and the art-critical establishment converging on a heroization of Duchamp.

Krystof draws a sharp distinction between painting and the history of images:

> Gerhard Richter's preoccupation with mirrors and glass pertains to painting, although occasionally there is an interplay in his work with the traditional symbolism of mirrors. In this respect, in addition to the glass objects themselves, the many photographs taken by the artist in his studio are very revealing—a conspicuous stage managing of mirror effects can often be observed in them.[34]

The term *experimentation* is preferable to *preoccupation*, especially as Krystof had ended the previous paragraph with the claim that Richter was attempting to rid his work of "any trace of subjective pathos." If there is pathos involved, it is in Richter's creation of a *Pathosformel*. Finally, Krystof turns her attention to the topic of affect:

> From the beginning, Gerhard Richter was interested in a new kind of painting. His consistent juxtaposition of figuration and abstraction, an approach that was interpreted early on as a denial of the slightest ideological influence and the expression of post-modern indifference, suggested Richter's characteristic detachment from the conventions of the medium.[35]

Although the term *detachment* (*Distanziertheit*) is not inaccurate, what its semantic and pragmatic contours are for Richter remain unexplored. What the term by itself does not adequately indicate, however, is the reasons for seeking such detachment—and what form it might take. By now it should be clear that I do not think this has anything to do with postmodern indifference. If anything, the power of Richter's work is precisely the search for a form of pathos of which indifference is a deficit term (and ideological representation the excess term) while the Neutral is the virtue term.

Element: Disappointment

By the time Roland Barthes joined the prestigious Collège de France (1976–77), he had come to the conclusion that given what he was attempting to think through—forms and practices to traverse the text of life without the modern as a guide—the traditional lecture form qua form would inevitably prove to be disappointing for himself and his audience. His three years of courses at the Collège are now published, and we can see how Barthes experimented with major modifications of the standard lecture albeit still set within the venue of the amphitheater of the Collège before an audience. Barthes's courses were organized and presented in fragments often grouped around specific terms, at times simply presented in alphabetical order. During his presentations there was a great deal of meandering and doubling back as well as reflections on that doubling back.

To the degree that a lecture was to be ordered and judged by its narrative flow and coherence, then Barthes's lectures were frustrating. Barthes was hyperconscious in his attempt to dismantle the lecture form but did not yet know what to replace it with—if it were possible to reformulate or remediate it. Thus, it is preferable to say that Barthes's lecture courses were not so much failures as experiments rife with disappointment. Presumably, both the speaker and his audience remained stimulated but unconsoled.

Eric Marty, who has edited Barthes's work posthumously, underscores this state of affairs.

> That disappointment is not only something Barthes anticipated but also, in a certain sense, something he sought. Clearly, the notion of disappointment is not to be understood in the usual sense but rather—to be fully Barthesian—in accordance with a *bathmology*, that is to say a science of degrees.[36]

This neologism was created by Barthes in 1975. The term is composed of ancient Greek βαθμός ("degree, step") and the suffix -logy (science). We can say with a certain admiration that Barthes was exercising the right and obligation to be inventive. Such efforts at invention carry with them no guarantees. More often than not, they will prove disappointing; more often than not does not mean, however, inevitably. Such rigorous and courageous groping is the way of science and art worthy of the name.

6

RESTIVE ENDINGS

Knowing how to end: Masters of the first rank are recognized by
the fact that in matters great and small they know how to find an
end perfectly, be it the end of a melody or a thought. [. . .] The
better of the second rank always get restless toward the end.
—**Friedrich Nietzsche**

Nietzsche's assertion is heartening as it provides a trope with which one
can comfort oneself. It is a relief during periods of wandering and *stultitia*
(troubled irresolution) to know that one might in due course arrive at the
heights of the second rank. The fiction of such an imagined and imaginary
station is reassuring for a number of reasons. The quotation from *The Gay
Science* that serves as this chapter's epigraph, paragraph 281, is followed
shortly by paragraph 283, "Preparatory Human Beings," in which Nietzsche
eagerly anticipates a more virile age in which heroism will be carried into
"the search for knowledge" and men will "wage wars for the sake of thoughts
and their consequences."[1]

A version of that challenge has been taken up throughout the twentieth
century and the first decade of the twenty-first with committed ardor by an
assortment of intellectual masters as well as hordes of lower-rank prophets,
sages, and technicians within the academy and within corporate, govern-
mental, religious, and other institutional walls. Nietzsche's hope is tragic;
seen with hindsight, it is at most a form of black comedy. In sum, it is hard to
imagine the eternal return of such a virile gay science as something even the
strongest could endure or that contemporary artists and thinkers of what-

ever rank should seriously consider finding a form to accommodate perfectly or otherwise.

Thinking, John Dewey held, arises from troubles in pragmatic situations. What attitude should a thinker adopt to deal with fraught practices and situations? Dewey's answer: a pragmatic and reconstructive one. "Pragmatic" means engaged directly in the troubled situation, and "reconstructive" means intervening with the goal of inflecting the situation so as to make it a milieu in which humans are more likely to flourish.

Foucault proposes a permanent and restive relation to politics (as well as to science and subjectivity) as a key anchor point in a mode of thinking he calls philosophical. Although the adjective "permanent" might seem innocuous, actually it is not. Working at establishing a permanent philosophical and anthropological relationship to politics, science, and the self is a lifelong undertaking that demands incessant attention and rectification. Such work requires the elaboration and practice of an array of the elements of a *technē tou biou* in the service of what Foucault called a *bios philosophikos* (philosophical life). Such a form of life, a mediated and monitored form of work on the self and others, entails the acceptance of a kind of perpetual discomfort with the situations one observes in close proximity—a permanent adjacency—but has the capacity to intervene in only in a restrictive and singular manner.

If the call for a permanent relationship might seem innocuous, the term *restive* cannot be elided with any ease. It is hard not to wonder what is at stake for Foucault in the use of this term. "Restive" has a similar semiotic range in both English and French: one core meaning is "recalcitrant." "Recalcitrant," it seems to me, however, conveys something that is too fixed and static. The German *widerspenstig*—unruly, against one's will—picks out a slightly different dimension of experience that unsettles what might otherwise be a general adolescent sulky or defiant stubbornness. However, even that stance still sounds too reactive and defensive to make "restive" such a valorized term. Yet another connotation in English—"uneasy and on the verge of resisting control"—is more enlightening. It indicates a mode of vigilance, an alert wariness.[2] Such vigilance should include caution about preemptory negativity. Vigilance requires attention to specifics and a suspension of unwarranted judgment. Judgment without inquiry renders one vulnerable to aligning with those who claim to know the significance of things, events, and situations in advance of their unfolding or assembling.

Finally, a "verge"' is a border, potentially available as a zone of adjacency. Thus, to say that "restive" means in part "on the verge of resisting control" evokes both an actively maintained observational position—an element of the repertoire of *technē tou biou*—and an *ēthos*—a dimension of a *bios philosophikos*. It should include finding or making a prime location to observe those resisting control or those seeking to exercise control. The dynamics and rationality of control, however, while demanding attention, are not necessarily the unique or even the most salient aspect of politics, science, or subjectivity. Power, after all, is productive.

Praemeditatio malorum: A Presumption of Evil

In his 1981–82 lectures at the Collège de France, peculiarly entitled "The Hermeneutics of the Subject," Foucault introduced an extended set of archaeological investigations into the techniques of the care of the self in the ancient world. Of direct interest here is his exploration of the linking of memory as a preeminent site of the integration of life and thought with a set of techniques that were grouped under the term *meletē*, translated as "meditation." The goal of this generalized apparatus connecting the present and memory through reasoned examination of one's actions was taken to be the medium through which an ethical life could be capacitated. An essential dimension, taken for granted and assumed, was that the future was unknowable, uncontrollable, and certain to bring with it dangers and evils. Regardless, nothing new and significant for the manner in which one led one's life was looming in the future, only more of the same. Stoic and other philosophers developed techniques, exercises, and practices for facing such a future, and consequently the past and the present.

The older significance of the term *meletē* has been covered over by subsequent Christian, Enlightenment, and modern uses, which differ in essential ways from the objects and objectives that Roman philosophers such as Seneca addressed. The Stoic scope of the term *meletē* is resolutely mundane in Max Weber's sense of "this-worldly." It refers to a set of practices formed to engage the everyday world and its perpetual, if sporadic, dangers, evils, and turbulence. These practices and their associated techniques were not designed to transcend this quotidian world for another beatific one, but to serve, instead, as a means of preparing oneself to face actual dangers so as to be able to lead, as best one could, a reasonable and composed life despite them. Given this perspective, meditation and its practices contributed an essential component of a form of life—bios—understood as a permanent preparation for a lifelong test of the self. This lifelong preparatory work afforded one the capacities for a testing of oneself and of what one thinks and how one practices what one thinks.

In the ancient world, both Greek and Roman, albeit in diverse manners, meditation was habitually linked to memory: truth in the form of recognition, the rent subject brought back to a repaired state of wholeness. The practices and exercises that Foucault groups under the term askēsis were designed to provide the equipment of true discourse on which one would be able to call for aid, for assistance, when the need arose. Foucault provides a crisp definition of *meletē*—the collection of practices, maxims, and exercises—as "the exercise of thought on thought." The constant goal of these practices was not epistemological, however, but rather one's self-transformation into an ethical subject, the test of oneself as the subject of truth. The challenge was to constitute the subject (oneself and others) as the subject of true knowledge and as a subject of right action. This permanent task was understood as being undertaken against and within the world that is perceived, recognized, and practiced as a test—the site of experience and an exercise in ethical being.

For those undertaking the practices of *meletē*—and, of course, most would not follow this rigorous path—the self-surveillance passed through an act of reason. But how was reason to be practiced as an element of *meletē*? "Reason is a gaze looking down, as it were, and a gaze that enables reason in its free employment to observe, check, judge, and evaluate what is taking place in the flow of representations and the flow of passions as the object of reason and the objective for reason to surveil, modulate, mediate and meditate on."[3]

A privileged domain of these exercises (and the manner in which memory was activated within them) was called the work of *praemeditatio malorum*, the premeditation or presumption of evils. Throughout ancient times, there was a constant and pervasive mistrust of the future. The future was a preoccupation; it preoccupied the mind, led away from memory, from recognition and identity. Training to prepare for nefarious events was required so as not to be taken off guard when they arrived. One of the ways one achieved this preparation was through an exhaustive review of evils. This preparatory work did not constitute a remedy; it would not prevent evils and demanding trials from taking place. Rather, it was a means of preparing oneself to face them in a reasonable, that is to say, composed manner. For example, Seneca wrote to a young friend: "to exhort you for the future, to lift your soul aloft against misfortune, to foresee her offensives not as possible events, but as bound to occur."[4] Fundamentally, all of this work was a way of sealing off the future as best one could.

The future was troubling. Thus, Plutarch argues that those who turn toward the future are *stulti*, foolish people who have forgotten or neglected to take care of the self. Those afflicted with *stultitia* are prey to the flow and overflow of representations of the external world and cannot discriminate among them. This lack of discernment, suffered by almost all of us, results in irresolution and restlessness. The *stulti* need help.

The ultimate problem, as these Stoic philosophers understood it, was that turning toward the future negated attention to the present. It followed that in order to ward off at least the part of troubles magnified by representations and passions of specific dimensions of the future as it appeared in the present, the future needed to be systematically nullified. Achieving such containment required a type of disciplined practice. The *praemeditatio malorum* was designed to achieve this nullification of the future through a reduction of the imagination, a restriction of its scope to the simple and stripped-down reality of the present. Practical exercises were designed to achieve this defensive disposition: since one could not know or work directly on the future, one had to work on what was available in the present, and what was available was imagination. If the site of *praemeditatio malorum* was the imagination—the site of the soul's trouble and agitation as concerns the future—one needed equipment to prepare oneself to diminish, ward off, or at least identify the source of these troubles. The *praemeditatio malorum* was a form of preparation "realized through the test of the non-reality of what we actualize in this exercise of thought."[5] Preparedness was the exercise of thought upon thought, in this case focalized in and on the imagination and the flow of representations and associated passions. It was a test of reality and of one's relationship to that reality.

Foucault and Gerhard Richter, an unlikely couple, provide different but serendipitously synergistic attempts in philosophy and art (as well as criticism and ethics more broadly) worthy not so much of direct emulation but as of possible aid for the *stulti*, those restless and troubled seekers filling Nietzsche's imaginary second ranks. Foucault and Richter can be seen to converge on a common problematization. Both move toward a reversal of recent and distant relations of the past and future—and their relationships with the present—as sites of *meletē*. Both seem to indicate in their work the worth of adopting this *topos* as one characteristic of how things might be better assembled today. Contrary to the perspective of the ancients, today for inquirers, the past is not the site of self-recognition, at least in a redemptive form. The problem of leaving the past behind in the proper manner requires work and discrimination, not simply negation; preparing for the future requires a tempered imagination and at least some glimmer of hope. How to achieve that tempering, preparation, and obdurate faith in work requires (among other things) a new form of *meletē*.

Richter or Foucault's goal is certainly not to simply erase or obliterate the past any more than to seal off the future—quite the contrary. In both cases, however, there is a distinctive kind of reduction of the present and the future involved in their work. There is an acute attention to the present. Sharpening and orienting that attention draws on extensive and intensive experience as well as a rich acquaintance with tradition understood archaeologically (and at times genealogically, perhaps more so in Richter's case). Furthermore, for both of these artists of contemporary life, the reduction performed both in and on the imagination is certainly equally a matter of taming the drive toward a free flow of representations and its associated theorizing, which knows in advance what is good or bad, right or wrong, in motion or in stasis.

NOTES

Introduction

The chapter epigraph is from Michel Foucault, "Pierre Boulez, l'écran traversé" (1982), in *Dits et écrits*, 4:220. "On croit volontiers qu'une culture s'attache plus à ses valeurs qu'à ses formes, que celles-ci, facilement, peuvent être modifiées, abandonnées, reprises; que seul le sens s'enracine profondément. C'est méconnaître combien les formes, quand elles se défont ou qu'elles naissent, ont pu provoquer d'étonnement ou susciter de haine; c'est méconnaître qu'on tient plus aux manières de voir, de dire, de faire et de penser qu'à ce qu'on voit, dit et fait. Le combat des formes en Occident a été aussi acharné, sinon plus, que celui des idées ou des valeurs. Mais les choses, au XXe siècle ont pris une allure singulière: c'est le 'formel' lui-même, c'est le travail réfléchi sur le système des formes qui est devenu un enjeu. Et un remarquable objet d'hostilités morales, de débats esthétiques et d'affrontements politiques." My translation.

1 Gilles Deleuze, *Pure Immanence*, 29. With sincere gratitude to Amir Eshel for his confidence and support.

2 Immanuel Kant, "Beantwortung der Frage: Was ist Aufklärung?" http://gutenberg .spiegel.de/buch/-3505/1. To paraphrase the beginning of the second paragraph of Kant's essay, most humans are content not to think for themselves because they are lazy and cowardly, even though nature has freed us to be intellectually self-reliant.

3 See Richter, *Gerhard Richter: Writings, 1961–2007*.

4 These distinctions are explored in Rabinow and Stavrianakis, *Designs on the Contemporary*.

5 Rabinow, *Marking Time*, 2.

6 Aby Warburg gave the term a specific meaning by using it conceptually to capture the sense of present but not thematized stylized motifs such as certain gestures that he found enduring from ancient Greek friezes through Botticelli's

paintings. In my inquiry, *Nachleben* refers to those objects, affects, and motions that are excluded or escape from modernist forms but nonetheless exist in the present. Identifying the presence of *Nachleben* in a situation contributes to the articulation of a contemporary mode. This practice foregrounds the challenge of bringing elements of the old and the new into a distinctive form thereby enhancing understanding and freeing one from constraints wrongly taken to be determinative.

7 The term was turned into a concept by the art historian Aby Warburg in his work on the history of style. It has a double sense: the attempt to give form to situations or moods of pathos and the only partial success of such attempts. As both the hybrid referent and concept, the term can play a powerful role in directing anthropological inquiry as well as decisions about an appropriate form of narration. Hence, deploying the term encompasses propositional, judgmental, and narrative registers. The practice of form-giving under the sign of pathos (as object and mood) contrasts with those of irony, comedy, and tragedy.

8 Didi-Huberman, *L'image survivante*, 42.

9 Clifford and Marcus, *Writing Culture*.

10 Buchloh, *Gerhard Richters* Birkenau-*Bilder*.

11 Ibid., 5.

12 Ibid., 7.

13 Ibid., 8–9.

14 Mark Godfrey, "A Curtain of Trees," in Godfrey and Serota, *Gerhard Richter: Panorama*.

15 In the 2015 exhibit at Baden-Baden, Richter changed the name of the production to "Birkenau." Birkenau was the largest of the six concentration camps where the Jewish genocide was carried out. It was built in 1940 and put into operation the following year. The Nazis began using the extermination system of gas chambers in the spring of 1942 and Birkenau was the last to cease their use in November 1944.

16 Buchloh, *Gerhard Richters* Birkenau-*Bilder*, 26.

17 Ibid., 28.

18 Ibid., 29.

19 Ibid., 12.

20 On these figures and their contemporaries, see Fore, *Modernism*.

21 Buchloh, *Gerhard Richters* Birkenau-*Bilder*, 20.

22 Mark Godfrey, *Abstraction and the Holocaust*, 9.

23 Ibid., 9.

24 Ibid.

25 Ibid., 12.

26 Ibid., 18.

27 Ibid., 13.

Chapter 1: Object

The chapter epigraph is from Adorno, *Minima Moralia*, 127.

1 Dewey, *Logic*, 122.
2 Hal Foster for the Editors, "Questionnaire," 3.
3 Molesworth, "Questionnaire," 112.
4 Ibid., 113.
5 Burton, "Questionnaire," 22.
6 Alberro, "Questionnaire," 57.
7 Maimon, "Questionnaire," 76.
8 Kwon, "Questionnaire," 14. One defining characteristic of the contemporary art scene is that many of the artists who fall into the category of contemporary art, either willingly or not, are alive and vocal about their own work, its meaning and interpretation, and who controls its distribution and significance: that is to say, its value. According to Grant Kester, "Rather than transmitting a preexisting content, expression takes place through an unfolding process among an ensemble of collaborative agents" ("Questionnaire," 9). In the view of Tim Griffin, "Contemporary art is all too ready to signal its own resistant stance, and so is perpetually at risk of merely becoming a marker of difference, distinguishing itself more in terms of style than subversiveness, and in terms of affect more than effect" ("Questionnaire," 61). Customization and specialization for niche audiences are its mark. The role of the auction markets is emphasized by Isabelle Graw: "The rise of the category 'contemporary art' to a label full of promise is directly related to developments in the auction markets. When in the 1980s, the houses began to set up entire departments for 'contemporary art' (the first auction at Christie's exclusively devoted to contemporary art took place in London on June 29, 1977), it amounted to an immense symbolic revaluation upward" ("Questionnaire," 119). And Tom McDonough asserts that "our understanding of the contemporary will have to include the process whereby over the last quarter century once commonly held goods—from air and water to our own subjective integrity—have been privatized in order to turn a profit" ("Questionnaire," 123).
9 Michaud, *L'Art à l'état gazeux*.
10 Another approach to these changes is provided by Clark, *Modernism*.
11 Michaud, *L'art à l'état gazeux*, x.
12 Ibid., 53. "Ce qui reste néanmoins, c'est le fait que toutes sortes de pratiques, *absolument toutes*, peuvent à un moment donné et dans certaines conditions faire partie de l'art contemporain."
13 Burton, "Questionnaire," 24.
14 The epigraph for this section is from Michel Foucault, "Il y a des moments dans la vie où la question de savoir si on peut penser autrement qu'on pense et percevoir autrement qu'on voit est indispensable pour continuer à regarder ou à réfléchir." In *Dits et écrits* (Paris: Gallimard, 2001), 2:1358–1380, quote from 1362.

15 Michel Foucault, "L'imagination du XIXᵉ siècle," *Dits et écrits*, 4:111. This was originally a piece in the 30 September 1980 edition of *Corriere della Sera*.

16 Ibid.

17 Ibid., 114.

18 Ibid., 112. "Mais faut-il comprendre de quel accompagnement il s'agit."

19 Ibid., 113. "Boulez a pris au sérieux l'idée wagnérienne d'un drame où musique et texte ne se répètent pas, ne disent pas chacun à sa manière la même chose; mais où l'orchestre, le chant, le jeu des acteurs, les tempos de la musique, les mouvements de la scène, les décors doivent se composer, comme des éléments partiales pour constituer, le temps de la représentation, une forme unique, un événement singulier."

20 Ibid., 115.

21 "Eric Clapton's Richter Sets a Record Price for any Living Artist at Auction."

22 Kulish, "Germans Embrace Artist as Home Grown Hero."

23 Richter, *Gerhard Richter: Writings, 1961–2007*, 212.

24 Ibid., 245–46.

25 Foucault, *Government of Self and Others*, 5.

26 Ibid., 5–6.

27 "Interview with Benjamin H. D. Buchloh, 1986," in *Gerhard Richter: Writings, 1961–2007*, 177–78.

28 "Interview with Benjamin H. D. Buchloh, 2004," in *Gerhard Richter: Writings, 1961–2007*, 494–95.

Chapter 2: Constellations

The chapter epigraph is from Hubertus Butin, "*Collection*," Gerhard Richter website. [31 min, 04 sec.] "Gerhard Richter: Editions" (video), https://www.gerhard-richter.com/en/videos/exhibitions/gerhard-richter-editions-55.

1 Darash and Rabinow, *Modes of Uncertainty*.

2 Foucault, *Hermeneutics of the Subject*, 182–83. Lecture of 3 February 1982, first hour. I have abbreviated the passage.

3 Storr, *Gerhard Richter: October 18, 1977*.

4 Dietmar Elger, *Gerhard Richter: A Life in Painting*.

5 Silverman, "Unfinished Business," Panorama Exhibition, Lecture 21 October 2011, https://www.gerhard-richter.com/en/videos/talks/unfinished-business-52. Hubertus Butin: https://www.gerhard-richter.com/en/videos/exhibitions/gerhard-richter-editions-55.

6 Hubertus Butin, "*Collection*," Gerhard Richter website.

7 Schwarz, "Variants, Cycles, and Series," 19. The epigraph for this section of chapter 2 is from Kluge, *L'utopie des sentiments*, 82, which I have translated from the French: "Il s'agit toujours d'une constellation. Une situation objective pour soi, c'est-à-dire le simple saisi instantané de son moment, ne contient pas en elle l'élément de son organisation, l'élément qui la rend concrète. C'est pourquoi la

découverte des situations objectives présuppose la production des moyens de leur production, soit les formes de production objectives."

8 Schwarz, "Variants, Series, Cycles," 33.

9 See Richter, *Gerhard Richter: Landscapes*.

10 Schwarz, "Variants, Series, Cycles," 20.

11 Ibid., 21.

12 For example, Buchloh et al., *Photography and Painting in the Work of Gerhard Richter*.

13 Richter, *Elbe: 1957*.

14 Schwarz, "Variants, Series, Cycles," 28.

15 Ibid., 21.

16 Ibid., 27.

17 Ibid., 28.

18 The epigraph for this section is from Schwarz, "Variants, Series, Cycles," 28.

19 *Gerhard Richter, Eis*, Köln: Verlag des Buchhandlung Walther König, 2011.

20 Schwarz, "Variants, Series, Cycles," 31.

21 Fried, *Absorption and Theatricality*.

22 The epigraph at the start of this section is from Mehring, *Blinky Palermo*, 174.

23 Palermo's real name was Peter Schwarze. He was born in Leipzig in 1943 and died in 1977.

24 Joseph Beuys, *The Reader*.

25 Mehring, *Blinky Palermo*.

26 Mehring, *Blinky Palermo*, 174.

27 Mehring, Nugent, and Sedyl, *Gerhard Richter: Early Work, 1951–1972*.

28 The series familiarity/trust/confidence is drawn from Niklas Luhmann, "Observation of the First and the Second Order."

29 Richter's interlocutor is Jonas Storsve. Richter, *Gerhard Richter: Text, Writings, Interviews and Letters, 1961–2007*, 272.

30 Mehring, *Blinky Palermo*, 174.

31 Ibid., 176.

32 Ibid., 180.

33 Ibid., 191.

34 Ibid., 198.

35 Ibid., 200.

36 Ibid., 203.

37 Ibid.

38 Ibid., 205.

39 Ibid., 206.

40 Ibid., 207.

41 Ibid., 212.

42 Ibid., 215.

43 Ibid., 182.

44 Ibid., 184–85, quoting Richter, interview with Robert Storr, in Storr, *Gerhard Richter*, 59.

45 The extract for this section is from Mark Godfrey, "From *Moderne Kunst* to *Entartete Kunst*," 121.

46 Elger, *Gerhard Richter*, 54–89.

47 Godfrey, "From *Moderne Kunst* to *Entartete Kunst*," 121.

48 Ibid., 118.

49 Ibid.

50 The following section draws directly from Elger, *Gerhard Richter*. More extensive and detailed examination can be found in the essays of Benjamin Buchloh and others. See also the synthetic overview of this period by Buchloh, Krauss, and Yves-Alain Blois. Josef Beuys was a central and important figure in this constellation. On Beuys, see Mesch and Michely, *Joseph Beuys*; Staeck and Steidl, *The Beuys Book*.

51 Elger, *Gerhard Richter*, 54.

52 Godfrey, "From *Moderne Kunst* to *Entartete Kunst*," 118.

53 Ibid., 125.

54 Ibid., 128.

55 Ibid., 125.

56 Ibid., 132.

57 Ibid., 135.

58 Elger, *Gerhard Richter*, 184.

59 Ibid., 184.

60 Ibid., 184–85.

61 The epigraph of this section is from "Interview with Jan Thorn-Prikker on the Work WAR CUT," in Richter, *Gerhard Richter: Writings, 1961–2007*, 463.

62 "ART; A Picture Is Worth 216 Newspaper Articles," *New York Times*, 4 July 2004.

63 Interview with Jan Thorn-Prikker, "On the Work War Cut" (2004), in Gerhard Richter, *Writings, 1961–2007* (New York: Distributed Art Publishers, 2009), 456–79.

Chapter 3: Assembling

The chapter epigraph is from Richter, *Gerhard Richter: Writings, 1961–2007*, 216.

1 Buchloh has announced the end of (modernist) art criticism. Buchloh, *Formalism and History*, xxvi.

2 Adorno, *Can One Live after Auschwitz*.

3 Storr, *Gerhard Richter: October 18, 1977*; Silverman, *Flesh of My Flesh*.

4 Richter, *Gerhard Richter: Writings, 1961–2007*, 180–82.

5 Storr, *Gerhard Richter: October 18, 1977*, 137.

6 The epigraph for this section is from Storr, *Gerhard Richter: October 18, 1977*, 68.

7 Quoted in ibid., 31.

8 Ibid., 28.

9 Ibid., 36.

10 Ibid., 130.

11 Storr, "Painting History—Painting Tragedy," 101.

12 Foucault, *Government of Self and Others*, 473.

13 Adorno, *Jargon of Authenticity*; Bourdieu, *L'ontologie politique de Martin Heidegger.*

14 Genette, *Narrative Discourse*, 182.

15 Ibid., 234.

16 Ibid.

17 Ibid.

18 Ibid., 236.

19 *"La pédagogie de Klee; Apprendre à déduire mais aussi à réduire les phénomènes. Tout le génie de Klee est là: à partir d'une problématique très simple et parvenir à une poétique d'une force remarquable où la problématique est totalement absorbée. Autrement dit, son principale de base est primordial, mais son imagination poétique, loin d'être appauvrie par la réflexion sur un problème technique, ne cesse au contraire de s'enrichir. L'imagination, cette faculté merveilleuse, ne fait rien d'autre, si on la laisse sans contrôle, que de prendre appui sur la mémoire. La mémoire fait ressort au jour des choses ressenties, entendues ou vues."* Boulez, *L'emploi de la technique*, 146–47.

20 Bloom, *Anxiety of Influence*, 141.

21 James D. Faubion, personal communication.

22 Storr, *Gerhard Richter: October 18, 1977*, 131.

23 The epigraph of this section is from Didi-Huberman, *Images in Spite of All*, 26. On the visible and the sayable, see Deleuze, *Foucault*, 56.

24 Ibid., 8.

25 Ibid., 24.

26 Ibid., 20.

27 Godfrey and Serota, *Gerhard Richter: Panorama*, 25.

28 Didi-Huberman, *Images in Spite of All*, 155.

29 Ibid., 171–72.

30 Godfrey, "A Curtain of Trees."

31 Krauss, *Optical Unconscious*, 254–56.

32 Godfrey, "Damaged Landscapes," 81.

33 Ibid., 83.

34 Adorno, *Can One Live after Auschwitz.*

35 Godfrey, "Damaged Landscapes," 83.

36 Ibid., 87.

37 Ibid.

38 "Translator's Note" in Didi-Huberman, *Images in Spite of All.*

39 http://www.etymonline.com/index.php?term=relieve.

40 Didi-Huberman, *Images in Spite of All*, 27.

41 Ibid., 34.

42 Ibid., 39.

43 Richter, "Notes 1989," in Richter, *Gerhard Richter: Writings, 1961–2007*, 213.

44 Storr, *September: A History Painting by Gerhard Richter*. The preliminary sketches for the painting were eventually exhibited at the Marian Goodman Gallery in New York in 2005.

45 Ibid., 38.

46 Ibid., 47.

47 Ibid., 48.

48 Hubertus Butin, "*Collection*," Gerhard Richter website. [31 min, 04 sec.] "Gerhard Richter: Editions" (video), https://www.gerhard-richter.com/en/videos /exhibitions/gerhard-richter-editions-55.

49 "From a Letter to Benjamin Buchloh, 23 May 1977," in Richter, *The Daily Practice of Painting*, 84.

50 Baudelaire, "The Painter of Modern Life," 401–2.

51 The epigraph of this section is a quotation from Max, "The Art of Conversation," 71.

52 Richter, "Notes, 1990," *Gerhard Richter: Writings, 1961–2007*, 218.

53 "From a Letter to Benjamin Buchloh, 23 May 1977," in Richter, *The Daily Practice of Painting*, 80–81.

54 The first epigraph of this section is from Alexander Kluge, 15 January 2015. The second epigraph is from Storr, *September*, 53–54. Borchard-Hume, "Dreh Dich Nicht Um—Don't Turn Around," 163–75, in Godfrey and Serota, *Gerhard Richter: Panorama*.

55 Schwarz, "Variants, Series, Cycles," 25.

56 Richter, "Notes 1986," *Gerhard Richter: Writings, 1961–2007*, 127.

57 Storr, *Gerhard Richter: Forty Years of Painting*, 76.

58 Borchard-Hume, "Dreh Dich Nicht Um—Don't Turn Around," 163–75.

Chapter 4: Composition

Nos gestes expressifs sont peut-être limitées, ou s'ils ne sont pas, ils sont fortement conditionnés par notre.

Lorsque nous sommes en train d'écrire un œuvre, nous somme à la fois en état de recherche et en état de référence. Reference, pas seulement du passé 'historique,' mais aussi par rapport à nous-même, à notre propre passé, à ce que nous avons découvert, à ce que nous avons établi provisoirement dans l'œuvre ou les œuvres précédentes. Certain traits nous semble soit inabouti, soit plus riches de possibilités que nous les avons vus ; ce sont des manques et des promesses que nous avons dans l'esprit alors que nous spéculons sur le futur immédiat.

Il y a donc reprise de certains chemins, voire de certains obsessions ; et notre sensibilité désire appréhender quelque chose de neuf tout en ne sachant pas comment l'aborder. Nous avons besoin d'amplifier, de détourner, de remodeler ; nous remettons en cause certains données. Malgré notre désir de projection dans le futur, c'est un passé immédiat ou lointain que nous mettons en jeu, que nous remettons en question. Avant même l'expression consciente du nouveau, il y a réflexion sur l'état présent, et déduction, extrapolation par rapport à cet état présent.

1 Guyot, *Racine, ou, L'alchimie du tragique*. In the theater, the emergence of pathos constitutes a break with classical tragedy. Scholars have argued convincingly that it was only with the sudden and unexpected collapse of the parameters of pity and fear as the affect poles of tragedy that experimentation with alternatives began to be undertaken. Thus, Racine, the paradigmatic classical tragedian in French theater, introduced pathos into his dramaturgy; its introduction did work to affect his audiences, but what they experienced ran against the grain of their expectations, upsetting and confusing them.

2 Mullan, *Sentiment and Sociability*; Barker-Benfield, *The Culture of Sensibility*; Watt, *The Rise of the Novel*.

3 Green, *Diderot's Writings on the Theatre*.

4 Butin, "Gerhard Richter: Editions" (video), https://www.gerhard-richter.com/en /videos/exhibitions/gerhard-richter-editions-55.

5 For example, *Gerhard Richter: Ohne Farbe / Without Color*.

6 Guillermet, "Chance Process and Chance Effects in Gerhard Richter's Over-painted Photographs."

7 The epigraph of this section is from Krauss, *Under Blue Cup*.

8 Ibid., 19.

9 Ibid., 18.

10 I will consistently use the term *medium-s* instead of *media* so as to distinguish how Krauss uses the term as opposed to its more common usage. I find this distinction clarifying.

11 Krauss, *Under Blue Cup*, 96.

12 Ibid., 98. Quotations from the Kentridge lecture are taken by Krauss from Carolyn Christov-Barkargiev, *William Kentridge* (Brussels: Palais des Beaux-Arts, 1998), 68.

13 "On structuralism's neutral axis, the combination of not memory and not forgetting would be installation." Krauss, *Under Blue Cup*, 128.

14 Ibid., 127–28.

15 Ibid., 99. She is citing Stanley Cavell, *The World Viewed* (Cambridge, MA: Harvard University Press, 1974), 104.

16 The epigraph of this section is from Adorno, *Minima Moralia*, 127.

17 Curley, "Gerhard Richter's Cold War Vision," 11.

18 Ibid.

19 Ibid., 29.

20 Adorno, *Minima Moralia*, 127.

21 Ibid., 126.

22 Ibid., 127–28.

23 Godfrey, "Damaged Landscapes," in Godfrey and Serota, *Gerhard Richter: Panorama*.

24 Ibid., 74.

25 Ibid., 75.

26 Ibid., 77.

27 Ibid., 75.

28 Ibid., 75.

29 Interview with Jan Thorn-Prikker in epigraph is from "On the War Cut" (2004), in Richter, *Writings, 1961–2007*, 456–79.

30 Buchloh, *Gerhard Richter*, 22.

31 Ibid., 15.

32 Ibid.

33 Ibid., 16.

34 Ibid., 18.

35 Ibid., 20–21.

36 Ibid., 28.

37 Ibid., 18.

38 Ibid., 20.

39 Ibid., 24.

40 Ibid., 27.

41 Ibid., 26.

42 Richter, *Writings, 1961–2007*, 218.

Chapter 5: Contemporary Consolations

The chapter epigraph is from Bernard Comment, *Roland Barthes, vers le neutre*, 159. The original reads: "Il s'agit, en somme, de montrer les *départs* de sens, non des *arrivées*."

1 Published as Barthes, *Le Neutre: Cours au Collège de France (1977–78)*. His last two courses were *La préparation du roman I: De la vie à l'oeuvre (1978–9)* and *La préparation du roman II: L'oeuvre comme volonté (1970–80)*.

2 Barthes, *Résumée du cours, Collège de France, 1977–78*. Cited in Comment, *Roland Barthes*, 261–62. "L'argument du cours a été la suivante: on a définit comme relevant du Neutre toute inflexion qui esquive ou déjoue la structure paradigmatique, oppositionnelle, du sens, et vise par conséquent à la suspension des données conflictuelles du discours. À travers les touches successives, des références diverses, et des digressions libres, on a essayé de faire comprendre que le Neutre ne correspondait pas forcement à la image plate, foncièrement dépréciée par le doxa, mais pouvait constituer une valeur active." Translation taken from Barthes, *The Neutral*, 211.

3 Barthes, *Le degré zéro de l'écriture*.

4 Comment, *Roland Barthes*, 163. "Dans ma thématique personnelle, le fragment

ne s'oppose pas paradigmatiquement à totalité, mais plutôt à la nappe, au continu, à ce qui coule d'une façon ininterrompue, infinie, et dont les formes caricaturales, les formes-farces, sont dans l'ordre du savoir la dissertation par exemple, ou le développement."

5 Ibid., 165. "On ajoutera que l'exigence de déliaison n'est pas le simple fait d'un dégout, ou d'une lassitude; elle est fondée politiquement."

6 Ibid. "Dévoiler, ce n'est pas tellement retirer le voile que de le dépiécer."

7 Ibid., 61. "Ou comment penser le hors-sens dans le langage alors que ce dernier est précisément le cadre du sens?"

8 Ibid. "Vers quoi l'on tend, ce vers quoi l'on ne peut que tendre, telle un 'horizon chimérique.' Non par une simple transgression donc (laquelle serait encore prisonnière du binaire pour/contre), mais une échappée hors du sens."

9 Roland Barthes, Leçon Inaugurale, Collège de France, 427–48, in Œuvres complètes V, Livres, textes, entretiens, 1977–1980.

10 Ibid., 38. "Le cours existe parce que il y a un désir de Neutre: un pathos."

11 Barthes, Le Neutre, 38. "Le Neutre comme désir met continûment en scène un paradoxe: comme objet, le Neutre, est suspension de la violence; comme désir il est violence." English translation: Barthes, The Neutral, 12.

12 Barthes, Le Neutre, 110. "La pensée du pathos (l'affectivité-actif) ne doit pas être cherchée du côté des métadiscours (-logies) mais au côté, un fois de plus, d'une philo-écriture, . . . ce pouvoir d'être affecté ne signifie pas nécessairement passivité mais affectivité, sensibilité, sentiment." English translation: Barthes, The Neutral, 77.

13 Barthes, Le Neutre, 229.

14 See http://plato.stanford.edu/entries/pyrrho/. Pyrrho appears to have lived from around 365–360 BCE until around 275–270 BCE.

15 Barthes, The Neutral, 111.

16 Ibid., 21.

17 Barthes, Le Neutre/The Neutral, course of 20 May 1978.

18 Barthes, Le Neutre, 195. "Je réunis sous le nom d'arrogance tous les gestes (de parole) qui constituent des discours d'intimidation, de sujétion, de domination, d'assertion, de superbe: qui se place sous l'autorité, la garantie d'une vérité dogmatique, ou d'une demande qui ne pense pas, ne conçoit le désir de l'autre." English translation: Barthes, The Neutral, 152.

19 Ibid., 214. "il est temps, c'est le moment."

20 Barthes, The Neutral, 170.

21 Ibid., 215.

22 Gerhard Richter in an interview with Alexander Kluge, in Gerhard Richter: Bildermacher, part of the series 10 vor 11, a show on the RTL television network, 18 March 2013. Quoted in Richter, Gerhard Richter: Editions 1965–2013, 12.

23 The epigraphs of this section are from 13 August 1977, Délibération, in Barthes, Le

bruissement de la langue, 408–9. "Tout d'un coup, il m'est devenu indifférent de ne pas être modern" and "Et comme un aveugle dont le doigt tâtonne sur le texte de la vie et reconnait de-ci, de-là, ce qui a déjà été dit."

24 Fœssel, *Le temps de la consolation*, 13. "La consolation appartient aux 'techniques de soi' qui permettent à celui qui souffre de se constituer en sujet actif de sa propre existence."

25 Ibid., 19. "Il s'agit d'élaborer des thèmes, des concepts ou des procédures qui s'imposent en lieu et place des anciens modelés de la consolation."

26 Ibid., 245. "La réconciliation abolit la souffrance dans la rétrospection: la consolation réplique à la souffrance de la souffrance en lui donnant les moyens de se raconter."

27 Quoted in ibid., 161. "L'idée selon laquelle les souvenirs seraient notre bien propre appartient à l'arsenal des consolations sentimentales et impuissantes."

28 Ibid., 137. "Le plus sûr chemin vers la désolation est celui qui ignore la désolation dont nous sommes issus."

29 Ibid., 273. "Nos consolations ont acquis le droit d'être inventives."

30 Ibid., 193. "La consolation des Modernes devient espérance."

31 Richter, "Notizen 1986," https://www.gerhard-richter.com/de/quotes. "Meine Landschaften sind ja nicht nur schön oder nostalgisch, romantisch oder klassisch anmutend wie verlorene Paradiese, sondern vor allem 'verlogen' (wenn ich auch nicht immer die Mittel fand, gerade das zu zeigen), und mit 'verlogen' meine ich die Verklärung, mit der wir die Natur ansehen, die Natur, die in all ihren Formen stets gegen uns ist, weil sie nicht Sinn, noch Gnade, noch Mitgefühl kennt, weil sie nichts kennt, absolut geistlos, das totale Gegenteil von uns ist, absolut unmenschlich ist."

32 Richter, *Daily Practice of Painting*, 18 March 1987, 127.

33 Krystof, "Visual Speculations," 81.

34 Ibid., 83.

35 Ibid., 85.

36 Éric Marty, foreword to Barthes, *How to Live Together*, xi.

Chapter 6: Restive Endings

The chapter epigraph is from Nietzsche, *The Gay Science*, 160.

1 Nietzsche, *The Gay Science*, 160.

2 For a phenomenology of vigilance, see Duval, *Temps et vigilance*.

3 Foucault, *Hermeneutics of the Subject*, 547.

4 Ibid., 470.

5 Ibid., 473.

BIBLIOGRAPHY

Adorno, Theodor. *Can One Live after Auschwitz: A Philosophic Reader*. Edited by Rolf Tiedemann. Stanford: Stanford University Press, 2003.

———. *The Jargon of Authenticity*. London: Routledge, 2002.

———. *Minima Moralia: Reflections from Damaged Life*. Translated by Edmund Jephcott. London: NLP, 1974.

Alberro, Alexander. "Questionnaire on 'The Contemporary.'" *October* 130 (Fall 2009): 55–60.

"ART; A Picture Is Worth 216 New Newspaper Articles." *New York Times*, 4 July 2004.

Barker-Benfield, G. J. *The Culture of Sensibility: Sex and Society in Eighteenth-Century Britain*. Chicago: University of Chicago Press, 1996.

Barthes, Roland. *How to Live Together: Novelistic Simulations of Some Everyday Spaces*. Translated by Kate Briggs. New York: Columbia University Press, 2013.

———. *Le bruissement de la langue*. Paris : Éditions du Seuil, 1984.

———. *Le degré zéro de l'écriture*. Paris: Éditions du Seuil, 1953.

———. *Le Neutre: Cours au Collège de France (1977–78)*. Edited by Thomas Clerc, Paris: Éditions du Seuil-IMEC, 2002.

———. *The Neutral: Lecture Course at the Collège de France, (1977–78)*. Translated by Rosalind E. Krauss and Denis Hollier. New York: Columbia University Press, 2005.

———. *Œuvres complètes V, Livres, textes, entretiens, 1977–1980*. Paris: Éditions du Seuil, 2002.

Baudelaire, Charles. "The Painter of Modern Life." In *Baudelaire: Selected Writings on Art and Artists*, translated by P. E. Charvet, 390–435. Cambridge: Cambridge University Press, 1972.

Beuys, Joseph. *The Reader*. Edited by Claudia Mesch and Viola Michely. London: IB Tauris, 2007.

Bloom, Harold. *The Anxiety of Influence: A Theory of Poetry*. Oxford: Oxford University Press, 1973.

Bourdieu, Pierre. *La distinction: Critique sociale du jugement*. Paris: Éditions de Minuit, 1979.

———. *L'ontologie politique de Martin Heidegger*. Paris: Les Éditions du Minuit, 1988.

Buchloh, Benjamin H. D. *Gerhard Richters* Birkenau-*Bilder*. Cologne: Verlag der Buchhandlung Walther König, 2016.

———. *Formalism and History: Models and Methods in Twentieth-Century Art*. Cambridge: MIT Press, 2015.

Buchloh, Benjamin H. D., Jean-François Chevrier, Armin Zweite, and Rainer Rochlitz. *Photography and Painting in the work of Gerhard Richter: Four Essays on Atlas*. Barcelona: Musea d'Art Contemporani, 1998.

Burton, Johanna. "Questionnaire on 'The Contemporary.'" *October* 130 (Fall 2009): 22–24.

Butin, Hubertus. Gerhard Richter: *Editions 1965–2011* (video), me Collections Room, Berlin, 2012. https://www.gerhard-richter.com/en/videos/exhibitions/gerhard -richter-editions-55.

Clark, T. J. *Farewell to an Idea: Episodes from the History of Modernism*. New Haven, CT: Yale University Press, 1999.

Comment, Bernard. *Roland Barthes, vers le neutre*. Paris: Christian Bourgeois, Éditeur, 1991.

Clifford, James, and Marcus, George, ed. *Writing Culture: The Poetics and Politics of Ethnography*. Berkeley: University of California Press, 1986.

Curley, John J. "Gerhard Richter's Cold War Vision." In *Gerhard Richter: Early Work, 1951–1972*. Edited by Christine Mehring, Jeanne Anne Nugent, and Jon Sedyl. Los Angeles: J. Paul Getty Museum, 2010.

Darash, Limor, and Paul Rabinow. *Modes of Uncertainty*. Chicago: University of Chicago Press, 2014.

Deleuze, Gilles. *Foucault*. Paris: Les Éditions du Minuit, Reprises, 2004.

———. *Pure Immanence: Essays on a Life*. Translated by Anne Boyman. New York: Zone Books, 2001.

Dewey, John. *Logic: The Theory of Inquiry*. Edited by Jo Ann Boydston. Carbondale: Southern Illinois University Press, 1991.

Didi-Huberman, Georges. *Images in Spite of All: Four Photographs from Auschwitz*. Chicago: University of Chicago Press, 2012.

———. *L'Image survivante: Histoire de l'art et temps des fantômes selon Aby Warburg*. Paris: Les Editions de Minuit, 2002.

Duval, Robert. *Temps et vigilance*. Paris: Vrin, 1990.

Elger, Dietmar. *Gerhard Richter: A Life in Painting*. Translated by Elizabeth M. Solaro. Chicago: University of Chicago Press, 2009.

"Eric Clapton's Richter Sets a Record Price for any Living Artist at Auction." *On Camera, Sotheby's*, 16 October 2012.

Foessel, Michael. *Le Temps de la consolation*. Paris: Editions du Seuil, 2015.

Fore, Devon. *Modernism: The Return of Representation*, Princeton: Princeton University Press, 2012.

Foster, Hal (for the Editors). "Questionnaire on 'The Contemporary.'" *October* 130 (Fall 2009): 3.

Foucault, Michel. *Dits et écrits*. Edited by Daniel Defert and François Ewald. 4 vols. Paris: Gallimard, 2001.

———. *The Hermeneutics of the Subject: Lectures at the Collège de France, 1981–1982*. Edited by Frédéric Gros. Translated by Graham Burchell. New York: Palgrave Macmillan, 2005.

———. "L'imagination du XIXe siècle." *Corriere della Sera*, 30 September 1980.

———. *The Government of Self and Others: Lectures at the Collège de France, 1982–1983*. Edited by Frédéric Gros. Translated by Graham Burchell. New York: Palgrave Macmillan, 2010.

Fried, Michael. *Absorption and Theatricality: Painting and the Beholder in the Age of Diderot*. Chicago: University of Chicago Press, 1980.

Genette, Gérard. *Figures III*. Paris: Éditions du Seuil, 1972.

———. *Narrative Discourse: An Essay in Method*. Translated by Jane Lewin. Ithaca, NY: Cornell University Press, 1980.

Godfrey, Mark. *Abstraction and the Holocaust*. New Haven, CT: Yale University Press, 2007.

———. "A Curtain of Trees" (video). In *Panorama: New Perspectives on Richter*. Symposium at Tate Modern, London, UK, 21 October 2011. https://www.gerhard -richter.com/en/videos/talks/a-curtain-of-trees-50.

———. "Damaged Landscapes." In *Gerhard Richter: Panorama*, edited by Mark Godfrey and Nicholas Serota, 73–89. New York: D.A.P./Distributed Art Publishers, 2011.

———. "From *Moderne Kunst* to *Entartete Kunst*: Polke and Abstraction." In *Alibis: Sigmar Polke 1963–2010*, edited by Kathy Halbreich, 118–43. New York: MoMA, 2014.

Godfrey, Mark, and Nicholas Serota, eds. *Gerhard Richter: Panorama*. New York: D.A.P./Distributed Art Publishers, 2011.

Graw, Isabelle. "Questionnaire on 'The Contemporary.'" *October* 130 (Fall 2009): 119–21.

Green, F. C. *Diderot's Writings on the Theatre*. Cambridge: Cambridge University Press, 2012.

Griffin, Tim. "Questionnaire on 'The Contemporary.'" *October* 130 (Fall 2009): 61–63.

Guillermet, Aline. "Chance Process and Chance Effects in Gerhard Richter's Over-painted Photographs." At *Panorama: New Perspectives on Richter*. Symposium at Tate Modern, London, UK. 21 October 2011. https://www.gerhard-richter.com/en /videos/talks/chance-process-and-chance-effects-51.

Guyot, Sylvaine, et al. *Racine, ou, L'alchimie du tragique: La Thébaïde, Britannicus, Mithridate*. Paris : PUF/CNED, 2010.

Kant, Immanuel. "Beantwortung der Frage: Was ist Aufklärung?" http://gutenberg .spiegel.de/buch/-3505/1.

Kester, Grant. "Questionnaire on 'The Contemporary.'" *October* 130 (Fall 2009): 7–9.

Kluge, Alexander, et al. *L'utopie des sentiments: Essais et histoires de cinéma*. Lyon: Presses universitaires de Lyon, 2014.

Krauss, Rosalind E. *The Optical Unconscious*. Cambridge, MA: MIT Press, 1994.

———. *Under Blue Cup*. Cambridge, MA: MIT Press, 2011.

Krystof, Doris. "Visual Speculations: Mirrors and Glass in the Work of Gerhard Richter." In *Gerhard Richter: Ohne Farbe / Without Color*, edited by Reinhard Spieler, pp. 78–85. Ostfildern, Ger.: Hatje Cantz in association with Museum Franz Gertsch.

Kulish, Nicholas. "Germans Embrace Artist as Home Grown Hero." *New York Times*, 19 February 2012.

Kwon, Miwon. "Questionnaire on 'The Contemporary.'" *October* 130 (Fall 2009): 13–15.

Luhmann, Niklas. "Observation of the First and the Second Order." *Art as a Social System*, 54–101. Stanford, CA: Stanford University Press, 2000.

Maimon, Vered. "Questionnaire on 'The Contemporary.'" *October* 130 (Fall 2009): 76–78.

Marty, Eric. Introduction to Barthes, Roland, *How to Live Together: Novelistic Simulations of Some Everyday Spaces*, by Roland Barthes. Translated by Kate Briggs. New York: Columbia University Press, 2013.

Max, D. T. "The Art of Conversation: The Curator Who Talked His Way to the Top." *New Yorker*, 8 December 2014, http://www.newyorker.com/magazine/2014/12/08 /art-conversation.

McDonough, Tom. "Questionnaire on 'The Contemporary.'" *October* 130 (Fall 2009): 122–24.

Mehring, Christine. *Blinky Palermo: Abstraction of an Era*. New Haven, CT: Yale University Press, 2008.

Mehring, Christine, Jeanne Anne Nugent, and Jon Sedyl, eds. *Gerhard Richter: Early Work, 1951–1972*. Los Angeles: J. Paul Getty Foundation, 2010.

Merleau-Ponty, Maurice. *L'œil et l'esprit*. Paris: Gallimard, 1985.

Mesch, Claudia, and Viola Michely, eds. *Joseph Beuys: The Reader*. Translated by Claudia Mesch and Viola Michely. Cambridge, MA: MIT Press, 2007.

Michaud, Yves. *L'art à l'état gazeux: Essai sur le triomphe de l'esthétique*. Paris: Éditions Stock, 2003.

Molesworth, Helen. "Questionnaire on 'The Contemporary.'" *October* 130 (Fall 2009): 111–16.

Mullan, John. *Sentiment and Sociability: The Language of Feeling in the Eighteenth Century*. Oxford: Clarendon Press, 1988.

Nietzsche, Friedrich. *The Gay Science*. Edited by Bernard Williams. Translated by Josefine Nauckhoff. Cambridge: Cambridge Texts in the History of Philosophy, 2001.

"Pyrrho." *Stanford Encyclopedia of Philosophy*. http://plato.stanford.edu/entries /pyrrho/.

Rabinow, Paul. *Marking Time: On the Anthropology of the Contemporary*. Princeton, NJ: Princeton University Press, 2008.

Rabinow, Paul, and Anthony Stavrianakis. *Designs on the Contemporary: Anthropological Tests*. Chicago: University of Chicago Press, 2014.

Richter, Gerhard. *The Daily Practice of Painting: Writings and Interviews, 1962–1993*. Translated by David Britt. Cambridge, MA: MIT Press, 1995.

———. *Elbe: 1957*. Gerhard Richter Archiv Dresden. Cologne: Verlag der Buchhandlung Walther König, 2009.

———. *Gerhard Richter: Editions 1965–2013*. Edited by Hubertus Butin, Stefan Gronert, and Thomas Olbricht. Ostfildern, Ger.: Hatje Cantz, 2014.

———. *Gerhard Richter: Landscapes*. Edited by Dietmar Elger. Ostfildern, Ger.: Hatje Cantz, 2002.

———. *Gerhard Richter: Text, Writings, Interviews and Letters, 1961–2007*. London: Thames and Hudson, 2009.

———. *Gerhard Richter: Writings, 1961–2007*. Edited by Dietmar Elger and Hans-Ulrich Obrist. New York: D.A.P./Distributed Art Publishers, 2009.

———. *Notes, 1990. Gerhard Richter: Writings, 1961–2007*. Edited by Dietmar Elger and Hans-Ulrich Obrist, 247–48. New York: D.A.P./Distributed Art Publishers, 2009.

———. *Text: Schriften und Interviews*. Edited by Hans-Ulrich Obrist. Frankfurt am Main: Insel, 1993.

Schwarz, Dieter. "Variants, Series, Cycles: Gerhard Richter's Use of Multiple Images." In *Gerhard Richter: Pictures/Series*. Edited by Hans-Ulrich Obrist. Ostfildern, Ger.: Hatje Cantz in association with Fondation Beyeler, Riehen/Basel, 2014.

Silverman, Kaja. *Flesh of My Flesh*. Palo Alto, CA: Stanford University Press, 2009.

Storr, Robert. *Gerhard Richter: Forty Years of Painting*, New York: Museum of Modern Art, 2002.

———. *Gerhard Richter: October 18, 1977*. New York: Museum of Modern Art, 2000.

———. "Painting History—Painting Tragedy." In *Gerhard Richter, October 18, 1977*, 119–42. New York: Museum of Modern Art, 2000.

———. *September: A History Painting by Gerhard Richter*. London: Tate, 2010.

Watt, Ian P. *The Rise of the Novel: Studies in Defoe, Richardson, and Fielding*. Berkeley: University of California Press, 2001.